Bill Rothman
3/7/88

FIELD GUIDE TO THE MAMMALS OF THE KRUGER NATIONAL PARK

FIELD GUIDE TO THE MAMMALS OF THE KRUGER NATIONAL PARK

U. DE V. PIENAAR
S.C.J. JOUBERT
A. HALL-MARTIN
G. DE GRAAFF
I.L. RAUTENBACH

Consultant editor I.L. Rautenbach

This book has been produced by C. Struik Publishers, Cape Town, in collaboration with the National Parks Board of Trustees, Pretoria.

C. Struik
Struik House
Oswald Pirow Street, Foreshore
8001 Cape Town

Reg. No: 80/02842/07

First published 1987

(Parts of this book derive from *The Small Mammals of the Kruger National Park* by U. de V. Pienaar, I.L. Rautenbach and G. de Graaff, published in 1980 by the National Parks Board of Trustees, Pretoria.)

Designed by: Sabine Chadwick
Edited by: John Comrie-Greig
Photoset by: McManus Bros (Pty) Ltd., Cape Town
Reproduction by: Unifoto (Pty) Ltd., Cape Town
Printed and bound by: National Book Printers, Parow, Cape

ISBN 0 86977 432 8

CONTENTS

FOREWORD

For many visitors to the Kruger National Park it is the spectacular array of large mammal species which constitutes the primary attraction. These large mammals have of course been well documented and illustrated in many publications. This is not the case, however, with the host of small mammal species which inhabit this vast wildlife sanctuary in the Transvaal Low-veld. The majority of these interesting small mammal species are rarely seen, even by professional biologists, and in many cases little is known of their life-histories and behaviour. Some are strictly nocturnal in habit and lie up or hide during the day in sheltered places; several are only found in areas remote from tourist roads; and still others are not regularly encountered because of their shy dispositions or because they are simply too small. The banana bat is a case in point: it is nocturnal, it has specialised habitat requirements, and with a head-and-body length of only four centimetres, it is one of the smallest mammals in the park.

In 1980 Drs. U. de V. Pienaar, I.L. Rautenbach and G. de Graaff compiled a book on the small mammals of the Park which proved popular with visitors. It was suggested that this should be followed up with a similar book on the larger mammals, a task undertaken by Drs. S.C.J. Joubert and A. Hall-Martin. When the necessary literary effort was completed, the well-known publishing firm, Struik Holdings, proposed that we do away with the artificial division of mammals into "small" and "large" and combine the two texts. The collation and editing of this work was carried out by Dr. I.L. Rautenbach, Curator of Mammals at the Transvaal Museum in Pretoria, resulting in this comprehensive book, *Field Guide to the Mammals of the Kruger National Park.*

The mammal fauna of southern Africa is of course remarkably rich. Excluding marine mammals, some 283 species have been recorded from the Subregion and of these 147 are known to occur within the boundaries of the Park, just over 50 per cent of the total. Although many of the smaller creatures are rare, or secretive, or both, it has proved possible to illustrate all but two of the species described in this book by means of photographs. There is no doubt in my mind that visitors who use this field guide will enhance their already memorable Kruger National Park experience.

It is with considerable pleasure therefore that I introduce this valuable interpretative aid to our visiting public.

A.M. BRYNARD
CHIEF DIRECTOR
NATIONAL PARKS BOARD OF TRUSTEES
REPUBLIC OF SOUTH AFRICA

ACKNOWLEDGEMENTS

The authors wish to express their appreciation to all those who have assisted over the years in collecting specimens of various species of small mammals and recording new distributional data for others. In this respect tribute is due to all the members of the Research Section, particularly to rangers †G.M. Adendorff, †F.D. Lowe, †P.J. v.d. Merwe, J.J. Kloppers, A.J. Espag, M. English, L.E. van Rooyen, P.J. Nel, L.J.J. Wagener, B.P. Lamprecht, D. Swart, †M.C. Mostert, P. Zway, M.C. Maritz. T. v. R. Yssel, E. Whitfield, T. Dearlove, J. Steyn, J. van Graan, B.P. Pretorius, J. Botha, P.J. van Staden, H.A. Schreiber and L. Hare; we should also like to thank †Mr. H.H. Mockford of Pafuri, Jannie Swart, Stephen Whitfield, and Danie and Pierre Pienaar.

Mrs. Jean Visser and Miss Sandra Weber performed the tedious task of copying the distribution maps from the original records in an exemplary manner.

On behalf of the National Parks Board we must also express our sincere thanks to the host of willing contributors who provided us with some of the excellent colour transparencies used to illustrate this book. Individual photographers are acknowledged below. Mrs. H.J. Keogh, formerly of the South African Institute for Medical Research, Johannesburg, kindly made available her collection of live rodents for photographing by officials of the Board.

The artwork for the two species illustrated by means of paintings is by C. Ebersohn.

Lastly, a large measure of thanks is also due to Mrs. M. Whyte, Mrs. S.S. de Jager and Mrs. M. van Niekerk (Nature Conservation, Skukuza) and to Miss T. Clutty (Transvaal Museum, Pretoria) for their faultless typing of the manuscript.

PHOTOGRAPHIC CREDITS

Don H. Bornman: 95
Gerald Cubitt: 99, 146
W. de Beer (National Parks Board): 74, 89, 94, 107, 111, 128, 138, 149 (left), 155 (right), 156 (left)
D. Engelbrecht: 124
Clem Haagner: 145
Ray Holing: 88
N.H.G. Jacobsen: 61, 83, 110, 152 (left)
W. Massyn (National Parks Board): 25, 26, 27 (left), 28 (left), 30, 31, 33, 34, 39, 44 (right), 45, 47 (above), 49, 52 (below), 53, 54, 56, 59, 60, 79, 81, 91, 121, 143, 147 (left), 149 (right), 150, 151, 152 (right), 153 (left), 154 (right), 155 (left), 157, 158, 159, 160, 161, 162, 163
Gus Mills: 86
National Parks Board: 119 (left)
P.J. Nel: 64
U. de V. Pienaar: 80
I.L. Rautenbach: 32, 35, 36, 37, 38, 40, 41, 42, 43, 44 (left), 46, 47 (below), 48, 50, 51, 52 (above), 55, 57, 58, 148, 153 (right), 154 (left), 156 (right)
Mitch Reardon: 69, 103, 131, 137 (left)
Dick Reucassel: 75, 77
G.A. Robinson: 72
Hazel Smithers: 70, 76, 78 (above)
Lorna Stanton: 29, 62, 66, 67, 73, 85, 96, 105, 137 (right), 139 (left), 141, 144
Lorna Stanton (National Parks Board): 63, 65, 71, 84, 87, 93, 97, 100, 104, 109, 113, 115, 116, 117, 119 (right), 120, 123, 125, 126, 127, 129, 133, 134, 136, 139 (right), 142
Peter Steyn: 106
C.T. Stuart: 78 (below), 82, 147 (right)
Pat Wolff: 92

INTRODUCTION

The Kruger National Park is internationally famous for the wide spectrum of wildlife protected within its borders. Its vertebrate fauna, for example, is recorded as comprising some 49 freshwater fish species, 33 amphibians, 114 reptiles, 507 birds and 147 mammals – a tally likely to rise still further as biological research continues. This rich array of animal life is made possible by the great variety of different habitats in the Park, each with its own unique plant community. Naturally enough, however, it is the particularly diverse large mammal community which has attracted the attention and interest of wildlife enthusiasts around the world, and which is the subject of this field guide.

With an area of nearly 20 000 square kilometres (1 948 528 hectares), the Kruger National Park is one of the world's largest proclaimed natural areas. It was gazetted as a national park on 31 May 1926, but has its origins in the "Gouvernement Wildtuin" (later the Sabi Game Reserve) established in 1898 by President Paul Kruger's "Zuid-Afrikaansche Republiek".

The Park falls within the summer rainfall climatic zone of southern Africa and receives most of its rain between September and March. The average annual rainfall for the area as a whole is 500 millimetres, but in fact it varies from under 400 millimetres in the extreme north to over 700 millimetres at Pretoriuskop in the south-west. Rainfall is, however, erratic and periods of prolonged drought alternate with very "wet" years when floods may occur, in a cyclic seven- to ten-year pattern. Summer temperatures are high, often exceeding 40 °C, while winter temperatures are moderate, with frost occurring infrequently and then only in low-lying areas.

Geologically, the Park may be divided into two sectors. In the undulating country in the west, the underlying formations are dominated by granites, while the fairly level plains of the east have a basalt foundation. Wedged between the granite and the basalt, and extending the full length of the Park from north to south, is a narrow strip of shale and Karoo sandstone. Mountainous areas are confined to the eastern border with Mozambique (where the Lebombo Mountains effectively separate the Park from the Mozambique coastal plains), the south-west corner of the Park between Malelane and Pretoriuskop, and some rugged, broken terrain to the north of Punda Maria. Inselbergs (isolated rocky hills) are scattered throughout the western districts.

Eight major rivers with their tributaries drain from west to east through the Park. Six of these are perennial and maintain a continuous flow of water even in drought years, but two are sandy rivers with only isolated pools during the dry (winter) season. Other sources of surface water include springs and pans, while the authorities have supplemented these natural water resources with a series of earthen and concrete-walled dams supplied by windmills and have constructed weirs on certain rivers to create artificial pools.

The different plant communities in the Kruger National Park result from the interaction of the various environmental factors such as climate, geology, soil type, topography and fire régime. Eight major vegetation zones are in fact recognised by Park biologists and in a more detailed survey a total of 36 "landscape types" have been identified. Each landscape type consists of a particular combination of floral communities and associated physical features. With this diversity of habitats it is perhaps not surprising that the Park should be host to such a wide range of mammal species.

The abundance of animal species, however, can also be seen as the consequence of the Park's large size and the fact that it includes two important transition zones. Not only does it sit astride the division between the more humid and moist eastern and northern areas on the one hand and the arid western areas on the other, but it also straddles the transition zone between the tropical and subtropical north and the more temperate south. This of course permits the existence of a greater variety of mammal species than would be the case if the environment fell into only one climatic zone. It also means, however, that the habitats in the Park are likely to be marginal to the requirements of certain mammals and this is in fact suggested by the low population densities of some species.

It is worth remembering that although the geographical distribution of mammals in an area such as the Kruger National Park is determined mainly by climatic conditions and by the adaptations of species to the different available environments, the *abundance* of a particular species in a particular habitat is dependent on a variety of factors; these are the availability of shelter, food and water, the degree of immunity to disease or to parasite infestation, the ability to avoid predation, and success in competition for food and space. It is this interrelationship of the animal and its environment which the ecologists of the National Parks Board seek to unravel in order to achieve the management objectives set by the Park authorities.

For the Kruger National Park is not left to manage itself. Large though it may be, it is not self-contained or self-sufficient; rivers may be poisoned or pumped dry before they enter the Park; man-introduced disease may run riot through a population of a rare species; or acid rain from factories hundreds of kilometres distant may upset the delicate chemistry of Park soils. Even the boundary fences, constructed to protect the Park, can obstruct the traditional migration patterns of certain ungulate species and cause unanticipated and unwanted ecological repercussions inside the Park.

In devising management strategies for the Park, biologists have taken particular note of its large size, the remarkable diversity of plant and animal species which it contains, and the relatively pristine state of the natural environment. Clearly the primary objective must be to ensure that the harmony which has existed for aeons between the living and non-living components of the Park, *viz.* the plants, the animals, the soil and the water, is maintained in perpetuity.

The management plans for the Kruger National Park are detailed and complex. There is, however, a strong emphasis on large mammals – often the first casualties of man's war upon nature – and to this end management strategies include reintroduction programmes for species which have for various reasons become locally extinct. They also cater for the manipulation of population numbers of certain species whenever and wherever it is deemed necessary.

For example, both the white and black rhinoceros have been reintroduced successfully to the Kruger National Park. A recent reintroduction exercise involving Lichtenstein's hartebeest from Malaŵi met with initial setbacks, but the remaining animals have settled in and are breeding. Several efforts have also been made in the last two decades to augment the ailing oribi and red duiker populations in the south-western areas. Owing to the secretive habits of these small antelope species and the low densities in which they occur, it has proved difficult to gauge the success of these operations. The same applies to the introduction of grey rhebok to an area of montane grassland in the hills near Malelane. Nevertheless, in all three cases sporadic sightings of young animals have indicated that the populations have been successfully established. On the other hand, attempts to strengthen the naturally occurring populations of suni in the northern and north-eastern districts of the Park have met with limited success simply because there have been difficulties in obtaining sufficient animals from areas in which they still occur.

Park authorities also have to cope with management problems resulting from the erratic, long-term rainfall fluctuations of the Transvaal Lowveld. Both herbivore and predator populations may react to the seven- to ten-year rainfall cycles by adjusting their population levels in a similarly cyclic manner, often slightly out of phase with the rainfall cycle. Such fluctuations can result in habitat destruction or local overutilisation of vegetation, or in the case of carnivores, excessive predation on rare or less abundant species. In these situations, park managers may have to intervene and manipulate animal numbers artificially.

Fencing of the Kruger National Park has also created management problems. This project commenced in 1960 with the construction of a game-proof fence along the western boundary to curb the spread of contagious livestock diseases from the Park to adjoining farmland. By the mid-1970s the fencing of the entire boundary had been completed – and movements of large mammals back and forth over the borders of the Park could no longer take place. This led to problems of overpopulation in some species and to excessive pressure on certain habitats. The more sensitive low-density mammal species suffered from this intensified competition for resources, and park managers were forced to step in with the necessary control measures. The species mainly affected are elephant, buffalo and hippopotamus. Park biologists have determined population "ceilings" for these three species, *viz.* 7 000-8 000 for elephant, 25 000-30 000 for buffalo and specified hippo populations for each of the perennial rivers.

The management of large-mammal populations, however, is an exceptionally complex task and clearly has to be backed by a comprehensive research programme. Scientists are therefore employed by the Parks Board to undertake a range of research projects aimed at unravelling the complex interrelationships of the key species of plant and animal in the Park ecosystems. One aspect of this research involves the monitoring of large-mammal numbers and each year a comprehensive aerial census of the large herbivore species is carried out in order to assess population trends. The carnivores are more difficult to monitor as they are secretive and predominantly nocturnal. Several research projects have nevertheless been undertaken on lion, leopard and spotted hyaena and from these studies and from subsequent monitoring programmes on predator-prey relationships, Park biologists have been able to refine and improve their management techniques for the ecosystem as a whole.

What of the smaller mammals? Some 65 per cent of the 147 mammal species recorded from the Park are classed as "small" mammals and it is a regrettable fact that our studies on these species are not nearly as advanced as those for the "large" mammals. Indeed, over the past six years intensive surveys have revealed the presence of 17 small terrestrial and bat species "new" to the Kruger National Park's checklist and it is likely that more will be discovered in the future. Some of the smaller mammals are considered to be rare or endangered in southern Africa and a number of species have been recorded in the Republic of South Africa only from the Park. In such cases particular attention is paid to research on their conservation status. The Pafuri area in the north of the Park proved to be especially rich in bat species, perhaps because the lush riparian forests provide a corridor of tropical vegetation into an otherwise semi-arid environment.

Small mammals such as rodents and insectivores may be insignificant in size and rarely seen, but when their high population numbers and faster metabolic rates are taken into account, it is clear that they may have a greater rôle in shaping the environment than many would give them credit for. It is unfortunate that other conservation priorities have to date prevented Park biologists from devoting the research attention to these species that they deserve. However, interest in small mammals is growing, and it is certain that these fascinating creatures will in future receive their due share of research effort.

It is our objective in this book to introduce the enthusiastic amateur naturalist to all the mammal denizens of this wildlife paradise. Space limitations allow us to include only some of the characteristic features of each species. The identification of species must therefore be achieved by comparing the animal seen with the illustrations provided. We have used the limited space available for the text to concentrate on aspects such as social behaviour and ecology of which the layman is generally less aware.

The scientific nomenclature and taxonomic arrangement in this field guide follow Meester *et al.* (1986). For popular names we also chose to follow the same authorities – a choice that reflects no more than personal preference.

SYSTEMATIC LIST OF MAMMALS IN THE KRUGER NATIONAL PARK

(Following Meester, Rautenbach, Dippenaar & Baker, 1986)

ORDER INSECTIVORA

Family Soricidae – **Shrews**

Small (2-35 g), unobtrusive animals primarily adapted to a diet of insects. Shrews have long and pointed snouts, the eyes are small but visible, whereas the ears are petite and the fur is short and dull. Most shrews have odoriferous musk glands on their flanks. The urogenital and anal apertures are often combined in a shallow cloaca. The shrew's high metabolic rate necessitates sporadic, frequent feeding bouts both by day and night to satisfy its voracious appetite (although the latter is often exaggerated in popular literature). Prefer environments with high humidity. Life expectancy is about 18 months. Gestation period 13-28 days.

Subfamily Crocidurinae

•*Crocidura hirta* Peters, 1852 – Lesser red musk shrew
•*Crocidura mariquensis* (A. Smith, 1844) – Swamp musk shrew
•*Crocidura cyanea* (Duvernoy, 1838) – Reddish-grey musk shrew
•*Crocidura silacea* Thomas, 1895 – Lesser grey-brown musk shrew
•*Crocidura fuscomurina* (Heuglin, 1865) – Tiny musk shrew
•*Suncus lixus* (Thomas, 1898) – Greater dwarf shrew

Family Erinaceidae – **Hedgehogs**

Small mammals, weighing up to 1 000 g. Most species of the subfamily Erinaceinae have spines, and these animals defend themselves by rolling in a tight ball with the spines erected. The eyes and ears are well developed, yet individuals appear to rely mainly on their sense of smell to detect food amongst debris. Snouts are elongated and pointed, and the tails shortish. Teeth are adapted for an omnivorous rather than an insectivorous diet, although animal prey forms a significant part of the diet. Testes abdominal. Crepuscular and nocturnal activity peaks. Eurasian representatives hibernate. Gestation period 34-39 days; average of five young born per female per season.

Subfamily Erinaceinae

•*Atelerix frontalis* (A. Smith, 1831) – Southern African hedgehog

Family Chrysochloridae – **Golden moles**

The torpedo-shaped body with its rudimentary tail is an adaptation to a fossorial life-style. Small, 10-250 g. Teeth adapted for an insectivorous diet. The eyes are rudimentary and covered with skin, whereas external ears are completely absent. The pointed snout is covered with a leathery pad. The skin is thick and tough and the short pelage has a metallic sheen. Forelimbs are powerfully built and the two central digits of the hands have enormous pointed claws for excavating underground burrows. Golden moles feed mostly underground on invertebrates, although some species forage to a lesser extent on the surface. Appears to be more active during summer, which is also the mating season. Average of two young per litter.
•*Calcochloris obtusirostris* (Peters, 1851) – Yellow golden mole
•*Amblysomus julianae* Meester, 1972 – Juliana's golden mole

ORDER CHIROPTERA

SUBORDER MEGACHIROPTERA

Family Pteropodidae – **Fruit bats**

Larger than insectivorous bats, the largest species having a wingspan of 165 centimetres. Often referred to as "flying foxes" owing to their larger size and fox-like faces. Fruit bats have large eyes, a moderately long snout, and simple ears lacking a tragus. They are adapted to a diet of fruit, pollen and nectar. The molar teeth are low and flat-crowned, an adaptation for crushing fruit. Ripe fruit is located by smell, and orientation is effected by means of the eyesight. They are not particularly manoeuvrable fliers, but are adroit tree-climbers in search of fruit. Do not hibernate. One or two offspring born annually per litter. Life expectancy up to 20 years.

Subfamily Pteropodinae

•*Epomophorus wahlbergi* (Sundevall, 1846) – Wahlberg's epauletted fruit bat
•*Epomophorus crypturus* Peters, 1852 – Peters's epauletted fruit bat
•*Rousettus aegyptiacus* (E. Geoffroy, 1810) – Egyptian fruit bat

SUBORDER MICROCHIROPTERA

Family Emballonuridae – **Tomb bats**

These handsome, small- to medium-sized bats typically inhabit the tropical and subtropical regions of the world. The distal portion of the tail is invariably free and resting on top of the long interfemoral membrane. Most species possess a glandular sac in the propatagium of the wing. The muzzle is plain (has no nose-leaves). The ears are often united at the base, and a tragus is present. Hindlimbs are slender. One young is born per litter annually.
•*Taphozous mauritianus* E. Geoffroy, 1818 – Mauritian tomb bat

Family Nycteridae – **Slit-faced bats**

These petite and fragile creatures are characterised by large ears and muzzles with complex cutaneous outgrowths along the margin of a deep longitudinal slit. The latter is probably associated with the "beaming" of ultrasonic pulses used in echolocation. The third finger has two phalanges. The long tail is included to the tip in the flying membrane and ends in a T-shaped cartilaginous process. Upper incisors bifid or trifid. Usually colonial, and roosts by day in dark cavities such as caves, hollow trees and aardvark holes. Although insects are also caught in the air, members of this family seem to feed largely on arthropods and arachnids that are gleaned from vegetation or from the ground.
•*Nycteris woodi* K. Andersen, 1914 – Wood's slit-faced bat
•*Nycteris thebaica* E. Geoffroy, 1813 – Egyptian slit-faced bat

Family Rhinolophidae – **Horseshoe bats**

Small to relatively large bats with medium-sized sharp-pointed ears. This family is unmistakable with the muzzles adorned with several conspicuous leaf-like cutaneous outgrowths resembling a horseshoe in outline. Unlike other bats, horseshoe bats echolocate with their mouths closed, and the sonar pulses are emitted through the nostrils and beamed by the complex nasal apparatus. The eyes are small and inconspicuous. Two teat-like processes are present abdominally in addition to two pectoral mammae. The wings are neatly folded around the body while roosting. Members of this family hibernate during winter, and many display migratory habits. They are very agile fliers. Although insects are at times caught in mid-air, horseshoe bats also glean arthropods from vegetation or from the ground. They regularly hunt by locating passing prey while hanging from a branch, from where they dart out to catch it, retiring to the perch to consume it. Most species are colonial and take refuge by day in dark humid cavities such as caves, attics, hollow trees, etc.
•*Rhinolophus hildebrandtii* Peters, 1878 – Hildebrandt's horseshoe bat
•*Rhinolophus fumigatus* Rüppell, 1842 – Rüppell's horseshoe bat

•*Rhinolophus clivosus* Cretzschmar, 1828 – Geoffroy's horseshoe bat
•*Rhinolophus darlingi* K. Andersen, 1905 – Darling's horseshoe bat
•*Rhinolophus landeri* Martin, 1838 – Lander's horseshoe bat
•*Rhinolophus simulator* K. Andersen, 1904 – Bushveld horseshoe bat
•*Rhinolophus swinnyi* Gough, 1908 – Swinny's horseshoe bat

Family Hipposideridae – **Leaf-nosed and trident bats**

Several authorities include the leaf-nosed bats in the family Rhinolophidae because of a great many similarities. Leaf-nosed and trident bats resemble horseshoe bats in that they also have cutaneous structures on the muzzles but differ in that these are less complex than in rhinolophids. Leaf-nosed bats have one fewer premolar tooth in either side of the lower jaw than rhinolophids, and differ also in the structure of the feet. They also have medium-sized, broad and pointed ears set widely separate on the head, and their eyes are small and inconspicuous. Like rhinolophids, members of this family are also colonial cave-dwellers, agile fliers capable of gleaning prey from vegetation or the ground, and display seasonal hibernating and migratory habits.
•*Hipposideros commersoni* (E. Geoffroy, 1813) – Commerson's leaf-nosed bat
•*Hipposideros caffer* (Sundevall, 1846) – Sundevall's leaf-nosed bat

Family Vespertilionidae – **Common bats**

Generally, vespertilionid bats are small (4-45 g), plain animals characterised by refinements of the flight apparatus which render them efficient, manoeuvrable fliers. It is the largest bat family, the most widely distributed over the world and it is encountered in the greatest diversity of habitats. The eyes are small, the muzzle is moderately elongated and it lacks nose-leaves. Nostrils and lips are plain. The ears are usually separate and rarely small, always with a well-developed tragus. Members of this large family display divergent behaviour patterns and habitat preferences. Mostly insectivorous, although some species specialise in preying on fish. Usually one, rarely two pairs of mammae. Between one and three offspring born per litter, and young are capable of flight at the age of one month. Newly born young are normally carried by the mothers during feeding forays. Life expectancy as much as 24 years.

Subfamily Miniopterinae

•*Miniopterus schreibersii* (Kuhl, 1819) – Schreibers's long-fingered bat

Subfamily Vespertilioninae

•*Myotis welwitschii* (Gray, 1866) – Welwitsch's hairy bat
•*Myotis tricolor* (Temminck, 1832) – Temminck's hairy bat
•*Myotis bocagei* (Peters, 1870) – Rufous hairy bat
•*Pipistrellus rueppellii* (Fischer, 1829) – Rüppell's bat
•*Pipistrellus kuhlii* (Kuhl, 1819) – Kuhl's pipistrelle
•*Pipistrellus anchietai* (Seabra, 1900) – Anchieta's pipistrelle
•*Pipistrellus rusticus* (Tomes, 1861) – Rusty bat
•*Pipistrellus nanus* (Peters, 1852) – Banana bat
•*Chalinolobus variegatus* (Tomes, 1861) – Butterfly bat
•*Laephotis botswanae* Setzer, 1971 – Botswana long-eared bat
•*Eptesicus hottentotus* (A. Smith, 1833) – Long-tailed serotine bat
•*Eptesicus melckorum* Roberts, 1919 – Melck's serotine bat
•*Eptesicus capensis* (A. Smith, 1829) – Cape serotine bat
•*Eptesicus zuluensis* Roberts, 1924 – Aloe bat
•*Scotophilus dinganii* (A. Smith, 1833) – Yellow house bat
•*Scotophilus borbonicus* (E. Geoffroy, 1803) – Lesser yellow house bat
•*Nycticeius schlieffenii* (Peters, 1859) – Schlieffen's bat

Subfamily Kerivoulinae

- *Kerivoula argentata* Tomes, 1861 – Damara woolly bat
- *Kerivoula lanosa* (A. Smith, 1847) – Lesser woolly bat

Family Molossidae – **Free-tailed bats**

Called free-tailed bats since the uropatagium is narrow, resulting in the terminal portion of the tail projecting freely beyond this membrane. The wings are long and narrow, with a tough, thick, leathery membrane. They are extremely fast fliers, capable of attaining speeds of 65 kilometres per hour or more, but are not particularly manoeuvrable and cannot take flight from the ground. They have, however, remarkably enduring flight abilities, and many stay on the wing for much of the night, foraging at high altitudes as far afield as 80 kilometres from the roost. Since they require to build up considerable speed before level flight is possible, they roost in places where a free-fall of at least a metre is possible. Free-tailed bats are of moderate size. The muzzles are broad, obtuse, obliquely truncate and usually sprinkled with hairs with spoon-shaped tips. Nostrils usually open on a pad. The lips are large and especially the upper lips are wrinkled. The legs are short, strong and muscular. The majority of species are colonial, and pass the day in narrow crevices in rocks, bridges, houses, etc. where they congregate in large numbers.

- *Tadarida fulminans* (Thomas, 1903) – Madagascar large free-tailed bat
- *Tadarida aegyptiaca* (E. Geoffroy, 1818) – Egyptian free-tailed bat
- *Tadarida ansorgei* (Thomas, 1913) – Ansorge's free-tailed bat
- *Tadarida pumila* (Cretzschmar, 1830-1831) – Little free-tailed bat
- *Tadarida midas* (Sundevall, 1843) – Midas free-tailed bat
- *Tadarida condylura* (A. Smith, 1833) – Angola free-tailed bat

ORDER PRIMATES

SUBORDER STREPSIRHINI

Family Lorisidae – **Bushbabies**

Bushbabies are nocturnal and arboreal. They are smallish, slender animals that appear more robust than they are, because of their long, dense, woolly pelts. They have rounded heads, and the large forward-facing eyes are a prominent feature. The ears are pointed, long and unusally mobile. The hands and feet are adapted for clutching in that the tips of the digits are enlarged and disc-like. These creatures are accomplished jumpers and the hindlegs are consequently long and powerful. Bushbabies are primarily insectivorous and carnivorous, although items such as eggs, fruit and resins are also eaten.

Subfamily Galaginae

- *Otolemur crassicaudatus* (E. Geoffroy, 1812) – Thick-tailed bushbaby
- *Galago moholi* A. Smith, 1836 – Lesser bushbaby

SUBORDER HAPLORHINI

Family Cercopithecidae – **Baboons and monkeys**

Medium- to large-sized (1,50-50 kg), terrestrial or semi-terrestrial primates with human-shaped bodies. Forelimbs are longer than hindlimbs. The pelage varies in colour, and covers the entire body except for the face, the circumanal region, the palms of the hands and the soles of the feet. Rostrum tends to be elongated and canines are enlarged. All the digits have flat nails and the thumb and large toes are opposable. Tails are normally long, but sometimes vestigial. Facial muscles are well developed, hence these animals are capable of a wide variety of facial expressions. Sense of smell poorly developed. Predominantly omnivorous. All species are social by nature.

Subfamily Cercopithecinae

•*Papio ursinus* (Kerr, 1792) – Chacma baboon
•*Cercopithecus aethiops* (Linnaeus, 1758) – Vervet monkey
•*Cercopithecus mitis* Wolf, 1822 – Samango monkey

ORDER CARNIVORA

Family Canidae – **Wild dog and jackals**

Small- to medium-sized carnivores (1,5-80 kg), with relatively long and distinctly bushy tails. A scent-gland is located dorsally at the base of the tail. The legs are long, usually with five toes on the forefeet and four on the hindfeet (the wild dog is the exception with four toes on all four feet). Each toe with a non-retractile, blunt and nearly straight claw. The facial part of the skull is elongated, and the ears are pointed and erect. The incisors are unspecialised, the canines long and powerful, the premolars sharp, the carnassials (shearing teeth) well developed, and the remaining molars have crushing surfaces. Adapted primarily to a carnivorous diet, but will take a wide variety of food items, including vegetable matter. Rely largely on smell and hearing, less so on sight. They are alert, intelligent and cunning in behaviour. Gestation period varies from 51 to 80 days (depending on body size). Females give birth to one litter per year.
•*Otocyon megalotis* (Desmarest, 1822) – Bat-eared fox
•*Lycaon pictus* (Temminck, 1820) – Wild dog
•*Canis adustus* Sundevall, 1846 – Side-striped jackal
•*Canis mesomelas* Schreber, 1775 – Black-backed jackal

Family Mustelidae – **Otters, badgers and weasels**

Small- to medium-sized (0,70-37 kg) carnivores. The incisors are unspecialised, canines elongated and sharp, carnassials normally well developed (in some instances adapted for crushing), and the premolars small and sometimes reduced in number. Facial region of the skull shortened, and the ears are small and rounded. The legs are short in relation to the body, and the claws are not fully retractile. Tails usually long. The anal scent-glands are well developed (particularly so in polecats). Colour white, brown or black, often with contrasting spots or stripes. Primarily flesh-eaters, but occasionally take vegetable matter, insects or honey. Mustelids are predominantly solitary, and have a reputation for being fierce, quick and often bloodthirsty. Some are aquatic, whereas other members are arboreal.

Subfamily Lutrinae

•*Aonyx capensis* (Schinz, 1821) – Clawless otter

Subfamily Mellivorinae

•*Mellivora capensis* (Schreber, 1776) – Honey badger

Subfamily Mustelinae

•*Ictonyx striatus* (Perry, 1810) – Striped polecat

Family Viverridae – **Civets, genets and mongooses**

The most diverse family in the order Carnivora. Small- to medium-sized (0,70-14 kg) carnivores. Ears small and rounded, the rostrum moderately long. The senses of smell, hearing and sight are well developed. The middle lower incisors are raised above the level of the other two, the canines are small and elongated, the premolars small, and the molars large. The legs are short in relation to the body. There are five toes on each foot in most species, but the thumbs and large toes are functionless and located well above the other digits. Claws are semi-retractile. Tail normally long and bushy, and the scent-glands mostly well developed. Most species are truly carnivorous, but some subsist on vegetable matter such as berries, nuts and bulbs. May be solitary or social, terrestrial or arboreal. Gestation period between 50 and 60 days, litters usually of 2-4 young.

Subfamily Viverrinae

- *Civettictis civetta* (Schreber, 1776) – Civet
- *Genetta genetta* (Linnaeus, 1758) – Small-spotted genet
- *Genetta tigrina* (Schreber, 1776) – Large-spotted genet

Subfamily Herpestinae

- *Paracynictis selousi* (De Winton, 1896) – Selous's mongoose
- *Herpestes ichneumon* (Linnaeus, 1758) – Large grey mongoose
- *Galerella sanguinea* (Rüppell, 1836) – Slender mongoose
- *Rhynchogale melleri* (Gray, 1865) – Meller's mongoose
- *Ichneumia albicauda* (G. Cuvier, 1829) – White-tailed mongoose
- *Atilax paludinosus* (G. Cuvier, 1829) – Water mongoose
- *Mungos mungo* (Gmelin, 1788) – Banded mongoose
- *Helogale parvula* (Sundevall, 1846) – Dwarf mongoose

Family Protelidae – **Aardwolf**

Recent research results validate the status of this monospecific family. In comparison with its closest allies (the hyaenas), the aardwolf is lightly built and only appears more formidable because it possesses a shaggy coat and a mane of long hair. The hair is erected when threatened, and the animal may also discharge a smelly fluid from the well-developed anal gland. The aardwolf is striped and has a bushy tail. It has a delicate skull with all teeth, except the canines, underdeveloped and conical. Tends to be solitary and nocturnal. Feeds exclusively on termites.

- *Proteles cristatus* (Sparrman, 1783) – Aardwolf

Family Hyaenidae – **Hyaenas**

Hyaenas are noted for their bone-crushing abilities, towards which end the premolar and molar teeth are strongly developed. The hindlimbs are characteristically shorter than the forelimbs, and there are only four toes on each forefoot. The claws are blunt and not retractile. Ears large and rounded; the tail of medium length and bushy; body colour brown with dark spots or stripes. A short mane is usually present. Hyaenas depend largely on their sense of smell. The gestation period is 90-110 days, with 2-4 young per litter. Primarily nocturnal scavengers, although the spotted hyaena is also an accomplished hunter.

- *Hyaena brunnea* Thunberg, 1820 – Brown hyaena
- *Crocuta crocuta* (Erxleben, 1777) – Spotted hyaena

Family Felidae – **Cats**

Cats are proficient killers and prey almost exclusively on higher vertebrates, sometimes considerably larger than themselves. Vary greatly in size (2,5-275 kg). The incisors are small, but the canines and carnassials are very well developed. The felid rostrum is short, which is a further adaptation to a powerful bite. The tongue is covered with numerous horny papillae which are directed backwards. There are five toes on the forefeet and four on the hindfeet, all with well-developed, sharp, strongly curved retractile claws. Cats typically hunt by sight.

- *Acinonyx jubatus* (Schreber, 1775) – Cheetah
- *Panthera pardus* (Linnaeus, 1758) – Leopard
- *Panthera leo* (Linnaeus, 1758) – Lion
- *Felis caracal* Schreber, 1776 – Caracal
- *Felis serval* Schreber, 1776 – Serval
- *Felis lybica* Forster, 1780 – African wild cat

ORDER PROBOSCIDEA

Family Elephantidae – **Elephants**

The African elephant is the largest (5 900 kg) of all land mammals. The massive skeleton weighs 15 per cent of the total body mass. The teeth are greatly specialised. The tusks of elephants are in fact modified third incisors of the upper jaw (all other incisors, upper and lower, have been lost), and consist of solid dentine with only a terminal enamel cap which is worn away at an early stage. There are no canines. The elongated cheek-teeth consist of three deciduous premolars and three deciduous molars, which succeed each other in the upper and lower jaws so that there are never more than one, or parts of two teeth per jaw functional at any one time. The fore- and hindfeet possess five toes, all of which are encased in a common integument but have distinct, short hoofs. The nose is extended in a long, muscular, flexible proboscis with the nostrils at the end. Ears greatly enlarged. The testes remain within the body cavity. The gestation period varies between 18 (Indian elephant) and 22 (African elephant) months. The young (normally one, rarely two) weighs 120 kg at birth. Longevity 50-60 years.
•*Loxodonta africana* (Blumenbach, 1797) – African elephant

ORDER PERISSODACTYLA

SUBORDER CERATOMORPHA

Family Rhinocerotidae – **Rhinoceroses**

Large (1 000 to 2 800 kg) and ponderous beasts with short and stout legs and a thin, short tail. In spite of their ungainly appearance, rhinoceroses are capable of moving rapidly. Forefeet have three or four digits and the hindfeet have three, each digit with a small basal hoof. The neck is short and thick, the head large and elongate, and concave in profile. The ears are erect, oval, slightly tufted and are posteriorly placed on the head. The unpaired horns are solid, of dermal origin (agglutinated fibres) and lack a bony core. The upper lip is prehensile to a greater or lesser extent and is used extensively when feeding. Keen senses of smelling and hearing, but vision is poorly developed. Gestation period 15-18 months. One calf born per cow.

Subfamily Dicerotinae

•*Ceratotherium simum* (Burchell, 1817) – White rhinoceros
•*Diceros bicornis* (Linnaeus, 1758) – Black rhinoceros

SUBORDER HIPPOMORPHA

Family Equidae – **Horses, zebras and asses**

Only the third (middle) digit is functional, and terminates in a hoof. Lateral digits are much reduced and non-functional. Large-sized, gregarious animals with long, slender limbs highly developed for cursorial gait. Cranium short and spacious, rostrum elongated. All species are hornless. Incisors are broad, the canines reduced, and the premolars and molars are strongly developed and high-crowned. Primarily grazers, using broad, sharp incisors aided by mobile lips to crop fodder. Following a gestation period of 330-350 days, a single (occasionally two) precocial young is born.
•*Equus burchellii* (Gray, 1824) – Burchell's zebra

ORDER HYRACOIDEA

Family Procaviidae – **Dassies**

Relatively small, rabbit-sized creatures; rather rodent-like in appearance despite their distant relationship to the ungulates. Upper incisors are long and grow from persistent pulps. The body is fairly compact and the tail is rudimentary. The forefoot has four toes and the hindfoot three, and all the digits are united to the bases of the last phalanges. All toes bear flattened nails except the second digit of the hindfoot which is clawed. The soles of the feet have enlarged

specialised elastic pads, which are kept moist by means of abundant skin-glands permitting cohesion to the slippery substrates of their preferred habitats. Diurnal, crepuscular and nocturnal animals living in colonies of up to 50 individuals. Herbivorous, but with a simple stomach. Digestion of plant material is aided by micro-organisms in a sac posterior to the stomach.
•*Procavia capensis* (Pallas, 1766) – Rock dassie
•*Heterohyrax brucei* (Gray, 1868) – Yellow-spotted rock dassie

ORDER TUBULIDENTATA

Family Orycteropodidae – **Aardvark**

A compact, medium-sized mammal (60-70 kg), with a long and thickened tail. The legs are short and stout, and the body is sparsely covered with bristle-like hairs. The hindfoot is five-toed, each toe with a robust claw adapted for digging. The skull, and particularly the snout, is elongated. Sense of smell highly developed and used for detecting food. Ears large, pointed and erect. Muzzle mobile, tongue highly tactile. Incisors and canines are lacking, and the columnar rootless cheek-teeth lack enamel but are surrounded by cement. This nocturnal animal feeds almost exclusively on termites. The sturdy legs and powerful claws tear open termite-mounds, and the long, sticky tongue gathers up the disturbed insects. Constructs large and deep burrows, which are often used by other animals as refuges.
•*Orycteropus afer* (Pallas, 1766) – Aardvark

ORDER ARTIODACTYLA

SUBORDER SUIFORMES

Family Suidae – **Pigs, hogs**

Medium to large, sparsely haired, robust animals with characteristically large upper canines which tend to curve out- and upwards to form sharp and dangerous tusks. The cheek-teeth are adapted for an omnivorous diet. The feet are four-toed; the stomach is two-chambered and simple, non-ruminating. The mobile snout is distally truncate, with a disc-like cartilage in the tip. Suids are adapted to grub or root for food in the soil.
•*Phacochoerus aethiopicus* (Pallas, 1766) – Warthog
•*Potamochoerus porcus* (Linnaeus, 1758) – Bushpig

Family Hippopotamidae – **Hippopotamuses**

Ungainly in appearance, hippopotamuses are capable of surprising speed and agility. Only two species in the family, the pygmy hippopotamus (180 kg) of tropical West Africa, and the hippopotamus (2 000 kg) occurring throughout most of Africa near suitable waters. The incisors and canines are tusk-like and sharp, and are in fact formidable weapons. All four toes on each of the four feet are employed in supporting the animal's weight. The stomach is complex, three-chambered and non-ruminating. The sparsely haired skin is about 5 cm thick and covered with special pores that secrete a pinkish, thick, oily substance to protect the skin in the water and from the dry atmosphere while on land. Ears are small. The mouth is large and the snout broad with dorsally located nostrils, the latter an adaptation to its aquatic life-style.
•*Hippopotamus amphibius* Linnaeus, 1758 – Hippopotamus

SUBORDER RUMINANTIA

Family Giraffidae – **Giraffe**

The necks are abnormally elongated, yet with only the usual mammalian complement of seven cervical vertebrae. The legs are long, and the back inclines upward from the loins to the withers. The apparent "horns" present in both sexes are in fact bony prominences of the frontal bones of the skull, covered with unmodified skin. The eyes and ears are large, whereas the lips are long and thin and the tongue is long and extensible. Giraffes have keen eyesight. Nostrils can be closed. Tail with terminal tuft. Giraffe bulls can weigh as much as 1 400 kg and cows 950 kg.

Can reach 55 kilometres per hour at full gallop. Whether walking or galloping, the legs of one side move simultaneously resulting in a rocking motion. Gestation period 14-15 months, one (rarely two) 102-kg calves being born at any time of the year.
•*Giraffa camelopardalis* (Linnaeus, 1758) – Giraffe

Family Bovidae – **Buffalo, antelope and gazelles**

This family includes the African and Asian antelope, the bison, sheep, goats and cattle, and is the most diverse group of ungulates. Many species inhabit grassland, and it is believed that the advanced dentition and limbs developed in association with grazing habits. The cheek-teeth are high-crowned and the upper canines absent or reduced. Unbranched horns always present in males and often in females, composed of a bony core covered with a keratin sheath: used to good effect as defensive weapons.

Subfamily Alcelaphinae

•*Connochaetes taurinus* (Burchell, 1823) – Blue wildebeest
•*Sigmoceros lichtensteinii* (Peters, 1849) – Lichtenstein's hartebeest
•*Damaliscus lunatus* (Burchell, 1823) – Sassaby

Subfamily Cephalophinae

•*Cephalophus natalensis* A. Smith, 1834 – Red duiker
•*Sylvicapra grimmia* (Linnaeus, 1758) – Common duiker

Subfamily Antilopinae

•*Oreotragus oreotragus* (Zimmermann, 1783) – Klipspringer
•*Ourebia ourebi* (Zimmermann, 1783) – Oribi
•*Raphicerus campestris* (Thunberg, 1811) – Steenbok
•*Raphicerus sharpei* Thomas, 1897 – Sharpe's grysbok
•*Neotragus moschatus* (Von Dueben, 1846) – Suni

Subfamily Aepycerotinae

•*Aepyceros melampus* (Lichtenstein, 1812) – Impala

Subfamily Peleinae

•*Pelea capreolus* (Forster, 1790) – Grey rhebok

Subfamily Hippotraginae

•*Hippotragus equinus* (Desmarest, 1804) – Roan antelope
•*Hippotragus niger* (Harris, 1838) – Sable

Subfamily Bovinae

•*Syncerus caffer* (Sparrman, 1779) – Buffalo
•*Tragelaphus strepsiceros* (Pallas, 1766) – Kudu
•*Tragelaphus angasii* Gray, 1849 – Nyala
•*Tragelaphus scriptus* (Pallas, 1766) – Bushbuck
•*Taurotragus oryx* (Pallas, 1766) – Eland

Subfamily Reduncinae

•*Redunca arundinum* (Boddaert, 1785) – Reedbuck
•*Redunca fulvorufula* (Afzelius, 1815) – Mountain reedbuck
•*Kobus ellipsiprymnus* (Ogilby, 1833) – Waterbuck

ORDER PHOLIDOTA

Family Manidae – **Pangolins**

Strange-looking animals that to the uninformed would appear more reptilian than mammalian. The entire body (except the abdomen) is covered with overlapping scales composed of agglutinated hair. Pangolins are moderate in size (5-25 kg), and lack teeth. The skull is elongated and slender. The protractile tongue is extremely long and tapered, and is a highly specialized organ employed in procuring food. The hands have three digits and the feet five, and each digit has a long recurved claw. Anal glands spray a foul-smelling secretion as a defence mechanism under duress.

•*Manis temminckii* Smuts, 1832 – Pangolin

ORDER RODENTIA

SUBORDER 'SCIUROMORPHA'

Family Sciuridae – **Squirrels**

A large and diverse group of rodents, found in most parts of the world. Vary in size from 7 to 60 cm head-and-body length. May be arboreal (*e.g.* the flying squirrel), terrestrial or even partly fossorial. Mostly diurnal, although some forms are nocturnal. Tail varies from longer than head and body and bushy, to about a third as long as head and body and short-haired. Five digits on hindfeet, four on front feet; fourth digit longest on each foot; a sharp claw on each digit. Ears usually relatively large. Basically herbivorous, feeding on leaves, fruit and nuts, but insects and small animals are also taken. Some species in temperate regions hibernate during winter.

Subfamily Sciurinae

•*Paraxerus cepapi* (A. Smith, 1836) – Tree squirrel

Family Pedetidae – **Springhare**

Fairly large rodents, restricted to arid and semi-arid sandy areas of East, Central and southern Africa. Skull massive with a broad and deep rostrum. Characterised by elongated and strong hindlegs, an adaptation for a bipedal jumping mode of locomotion when disturbed. The clawed forefeet are small, but normally springhares walk on all four legs when foraging and when moving slowly. The hindfeet are elongated, whereas the digits have strong and flattened claws adapted for digging. The long furred tail has a tufted distal section. Nocturnal. Constructs elaborate burrow-systems. Ears large, and the ear opening is guarded by a tragus that closes over the opening when the animal is digging.

•*Pedetes capensis* (Forster, 1778) – Springhare

SUBORDER 'HYSTRICOMORPHA'

Family Hystricidae – **Porcupines**

The Old World porcupines are large, heavy-set rodents with a mass of up to 30 kg. Some of the hairs are modified into stiff, long, sharp spines which are erected as a defence mechanism under duress. Some of the quills are open-ended and shorter, and are rattled when the animal is disturbed. The quills are often conspicuously marked with black and white bands, and this visual signal together with the rattling of open-ended quills serves to deter predators. The neck muscles are strongly developed, and the feet are five-toed with smooth soles. Feed on plant material, often the bark of trees. Nocturnal, terrestrial, and dig extensive burrow-systems.

•*Hystrix africaeaustralis* Peters, 1852 – Porcupine

Family Thryonomyidae – **Cane-rats**

This family comprises only one genus with two species, restricted to the sub-Saharan region of Africa. Large rodents with a mass of 4-9 kg, and with a coarse and grizzled pelage. Skull mas-

sive. The snout is blunt and the ears and tail are short. The fifth digit of the forefoot is vestigial, and the claws of the other digits are strong and adapted for digging. These herbivorous rodents are restricted to the vicinity of water, and are good swimmers.
•*Thryonomys swinderianus* (Temminck, 1827) – Greater cane-rat

Family Bathyergidae – **Rodent moles**

This unusual family contains five genera and approximately nine species, and is restricted to Africa. Small rodents (up to 330 mm head-and-body length) adapted to a highly fossorial lifestyle. Construct extensive burrow-systems and seldom venture above ground. Herbivorous. The body is cigar-shaped, the neck is muscular, and the limbs are short and robust with long and curved claws. The eyes are underdeveloped and small, and the ears lack pinnae. The skull is robust, with the incisors extremely powerful and procumbent in all species. The animal burrows mainly with the incisors. The lips close tightly behind the incisors to prevent dirt entering the mouth while burrowing. The tail is short.
•*Cryptomys hottentotus* (Lesson, 1826) – Common molerat

SUBORDER 'MYOMORPHA'

Family Muridae – **Rats, mice and gerbils**

The second-largest family of rodents, and as a result of introductions by man certain species are virtually cosmopolitan in range. Many rodents are commensal with man and are therefore of great (negative) economic importance. Vary in size from 4 to 1 000 g. The tail is normally naked and scaly, although some forms have furred tails. The feet have retained all of the digits, but the pollex is rudimentary. Soles of feet naked. Morphology, habits, habitat preferences and diets vary greatly, as could be expected in such a large group.

Subfamily Otomyinae

•*Otomys angoniensis* Wroughton, 1906 – Angoni vlei rat

Subfamily Gerbillinae

•*Tatera leucogaster* (Peters, 1852) – Bushveld gerbil

Subfamily Cricetomyinae

•*Cricetomys gambianus* Waterhouse, 1840 – Giant rat
•*Saccostomus campestris* Peters, 1846 – Pouched mouse

Subfamily Dendromurinae

•*Dendromus melanotis* A. Smith, 1834 – Grey climbing mouse
•*Dendromus mystacalis* Heuglin, 1863 – Chestnut climbing mouse
•*Steatomys pratensis* Peters, 1846 – Fat mouse

Subfamily Murinae

•*Acomys spinosissimus* (Peters, 1852) – Common spiny mouse
•*Lemniscomys rosalia* (Thomas, 1904) – Single-striped mouse
•*Dasymys incomtus* (Sundevall, 1847) – Water rat
•*Grammomys dolichurus* (Smuts, 1832) – Woodland mouse
•*Mus musculus* Linnaeus, 1758 – House mouse
•*Mus minutoides* A. Smith, 1834 – Pygmy mouse
•*Mastomys natalensis* (A. Smith, 1834) – Natal multimammate mouse
•*Mastomys coucha* (A. Smith, 1836) – Multimammate mouse
•*Thallomys paedulcus* (Sundevall, 1846) – Tree rat
•*Aethomys chrysophilus* (De Winton, 1897) – Red veld rat

•*Aethomys namaquensis* (A. Smith, 1834) – Namaqua rock mouse
•*Rattus rattus* (Linnaeus, 1758) – House rat

Family Gliridae – **Dormice**

A family of Old World rodents adapted for climbing, hence they are normally tree- or rock-living. The limbs and digits are fairly short, whereas the short claws are curved and used for climbing. Dormice are characterised by long bushy tails, prominent eyes and soft fur. They differ from other rodent families in the detailed characteristics of the teeth as well as the structure of the skull, which has a smooth, rounded braincase, a short rostrum and large orbits. Dormice hibernate during winter in cold areas. A unique feature of dormice is the facility with which they lose or break their tails on rough handling, coupled with their limited powers of regenerating portions of tail tissue after injury.
•*Graphiurus murinus* (Desmarest, 1822) – Woodland dormouse

ORDER LAGOMORPHA

Family Leporidae – **Hares**

Although lagomorphs superficially resemble rodents in appearance, particularly with their large, ever-growing and procumbent incisors, they have no clear relationships to other mammalian orders. Whereas rodents have only one pair of upper and lower incisors, lagomorphs have two upper pairs. The cheek-teeth are high-crowned and rootless, an adaptation to an entirely herbivorous diet. The skulls are highly fenestrated and the clavicle is rudimentary. The front feet have five digits and the hindfeet either four or five. The soles of the feet are covered with hair. The tail is short and furred. The legs are elongated and articulation is especially adapted for particularly swift movement.
•*Lepus capensis* Linnaeus, 1758 – Cape hare
•*Lepus saxatilis* F. Cuvier, 1823 – Scrub hare
•*Pronolagus crassicaudatus* (I. Geoffroy, 1832) – Natal red hare

ORDER MACROSCELIDEA

Family Macroscelididae – **Elephant-shrews**

The long, slender, sensitive and moveable snout is the most outstanding characteristic of these small (30-230 g) and delicate creatures. Teeth adapted for a diet of insects. Large ears and eyes, the latter in most species accentuated by a pale ring. The hindlimbs and feet are elongated, the forelimbs short and slender. They normally walk or run, but when disturbed move with leaps and bounds. Tail as long as body. Fur soft and moderately long. A naked, black gland is situated at the base of the tail. Testes are abdominal. Average of two young per litter.

Subfamily Macroscelidinae

•*Petrodromus tetradactylus* Peters, 1846 – Four-toed elephant-shrew
•*Elephantulus brachyrhynchus* (A. Smith, 1836) – Short-snouted elephant-shrew
•*Elephantulus myurus* Thomas & Schwann, 1906 – Rock elephant-shrew

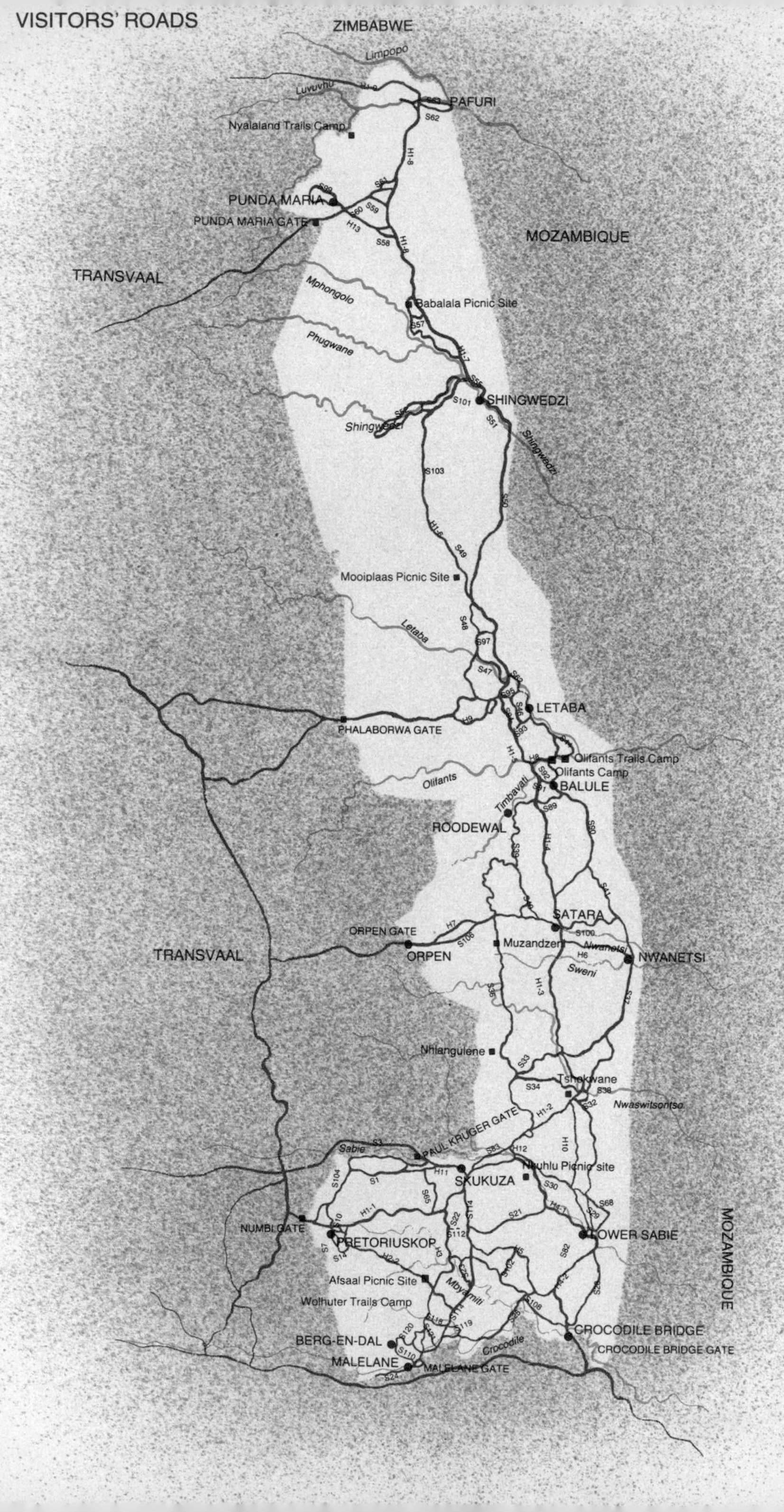
VISITORS' ROADS
ZIMBABWE
Limpopo
Luvuvhu
PAFURI
Nyalaland Trails Camp
PUNDA MARIA
PUNDA MARIA GATE
MOZAMBIQUE
TRANSVAAL
Mphongolo
Babalala Picnic Site
Phugwane
SHINGWEDZI
Shingwedzi
Mooiplaas Picnic Site
Letaba
LETABA
PHALABORWA GATE
Olifants Trails Camp
Olifants Camp
Olifants
BALULE
Timbavati
ROODEWAL
SATARA
ORPEN GATE
ORPEN
Muzandzeni
NWANETSI
TRANSVAAL
Sweni
Nhlangulene
Tshokwane
Nwaswitsontso
PAUL KRUGER GATE
Sabie
SKUKUZA
Nkuhlu Picnic site
NUMBI GATE
PRETORIUSKOP
LOWER SABIE
MOZAMBIQUE
Afsaal Picnic Site
Mbyamiti
Wolhuter Trails Camp
CROCODILE BRIDGE
BERG-EN-DAL
CROCODILE BRIDGE GATE
Crocodile
MALELANE
MALELANE GATE

ORDER INSECTIVORA

Family Soricidae

Shrews

Lesser red musk shrew

Crocidura hirta

Kleiner rooiskeerbek

Distribution: The lesser red musk shrew is generally distributed throughout the Park in suitable habitat. Judging from the number of skull remnants found in the pellets of barn owls, this is the most common shrew species in the Park.

Habitat: It appears to have a wide habitat tolerance, occurring in a variety of plant associations and at different altitudes. An essential requirement appears to be cover of some sort, including matted vegetation, piles of rocks or debris, fallen trees, holes in the ground or termite-mounds.

Habits: These shrews are mainly nocturnal, but have also been captured during the day. Like all other shrews, the lesser red musk shrew has a high metabolic rate, necessitating regular feeding forays. Although normally solitary in the wild, captive animals may live amicably together in groups of two or more, provided they are introduced at the same time into the cage. New introductions into an occupied cage may be regarded as intruders and ferocious fighting will result. They appear to prefer nests constructed of grass or other soft material, but also burrow occasionally.

Diet: Captive lesser red musk shrews have been maintained for considerable periods on a diet of ground beef, while beef liver is also eaten with relish. Apart from this they accept such items as earthworms, meal-worms, mantises, crickets, termites, beetles, long-horned grasshoppers, moths and even the carcasses of bats and rodents. Cannibalism is occasionally encountered. They have enormous appetites and consume as much as half their own mass in food daily.

Breeding: Captive animals have produced young during the period January to April, whereas field observations indicate offspring are born during summer from September to May. Litter size varies from one to nine, and the gestation period appears to be about 18 days.

Lesser red musk shrew

Swamp musk shrew *Crocidura mariquensis*
Vleiskeerbek

Distribution: The only record of occurrence for this species within the Kruger National Park is a series of eight specimens taken on swampy ground around the edge of the Matukwala Dam in the Punda Maria Section. It is likely to be found elsewhere in the Park where suitable habitat exists.
Habitat: It is narrowly confined to moist habitat amongst dense tangled vegetation and semi-aquatic reeds along streams and on the fringes of swamps. As a result of its particular habitat requirements, the swamp musk shrew is very susceptible to droughts.
Habits: These characteristically dark-coloured shrews are active both by day and night, although trapping results indicate a possible activity peak during the hours of darkness. The runways of vlei rats and water rats are utilised for foraging purposes. They appear to construct a grass-lined nest above ground rather than a subterranean burrow, which in optimum habitat conditions would be subject to flooding.
Diet: They are insectivorous, but are particularly partial to snails which abound in the moist environment of their preferred habitat.
Breeding: The young are born during the warmer, wetter months of summer from August to April. Litter sizes vary from two to five.

Reddish-grey musk shrew *Crocidura cyanea*
Rooigrysskeerbek

Distribution: A number of specimens of this species have been collected at Malelane, at Crocodile Bridge on the north bank of the Crocodile River, and at Punda Maria as well as at several localities in the Pafuri district. Its wide distribution through most of sub-Saharan Africa suggests that the reddish-grey musk shrew will probably be found to occur throughout the Park.
Habitat: This shrew has a wide habitat tolerance, but is more often encoun-

Swamp musk shrew

Reddish-grey musk shrew Lesser grey-brown musk shrew

tered in savanna or grassland provided there is sufficient cover available in the form of dense grass, accumulated plant debris, piles of rocks or dense scrub thickets.

Habits: Individuals of this species exhibit both diurnal and nocturnal activity and are ferocious and efficient hunters. The prey is consumed on the spot. Little is known of their nesting habits, and although their social habits are also virtually unknown, they are believed to be predominantly solitary.

Breeding: The little information which is available suggests that reproduction occurs during summer between the months of October and March. Litter sizes vary from two to six.

Lesser grey-brown musk shrew *Crocidura silacea*

Kleiner grysbruinskeerbek

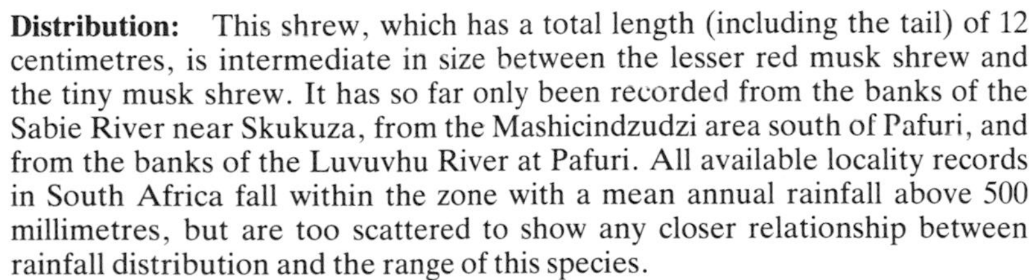

Distribution: This shrew, which has a total length (including the tail) of 12 centimetres, is intermediate in size between the lesser red musk shrew and the tiny musk shrew. It has so far only been recorded from the banks of the Sabie River near Skukuza, from the Mashicindzudzi area south of Pafuri, and from the banks of the Luvuvhu River at Pafuri. All available locality records in South Africa fall within the zone with a mean annual rainfall above 500 millimetres, but are too scattered to show any closer relationship between rainfall distribution and the range of this species.

Habitat: Several different vegetation types are occupied, including coastal forest-savanna mosaic, montane forest, riverine forest, undifferentiated montane communities, woodland and savannas as well as temperate and subtropical grassland. It has been collected under trees, in old timber, under rocks and stones, in riverine grassland and in the open veld.

Habits: Apart from its being primarily nocturnal little is known of its social, feeding, nesting and breeding habits.

Breeding: No information is available.

Tiny musk shrew

Greater dwarf shrew

Tiny musk shrew
Crocidura fuscomurina

Dwergskeerbek

Distribution: The distribution of this species is very similar to that of the lesser red musk shrew and it occurs throughout the entire Park. It appears to be less numerous, however, and is rarely captured in traps or encountered as skeletal remains in owl pellets.
Habitat: It is found in both savanna and woodland and appears to require some cover such as debris, fallen trees, wood-piles or dense grass clumps.
Habits: The presence of tiny musk shrew remains in regurgitated barn owl (*Tyto alba*) pellets indicates nocturnal activity, although it is expected to be active also during the day-time. This species apparently favours areas with sandy soil near water but little is known of its feeding habits.
Breeding: Two newly born young were found at Skukuza during December and a pregnant female captured in November contained four foetuses. The young are born naked, and start venturing from the nest at the age of 17 days. "Caravanning", *i.e.* where the litter trails the mother in line astern, each sibling in turn biting on to the rump of the one preceding, has been observed in captivity.

Greater dwarf shrew
Suncus lixus

Groter dwergskeerbek

Skull remnants of shrews retrieved from regurgitated owl pellets found at Pretoriuskop, Skukuza Koppies, Nwanetsi, Shilowa and Malahlapanga, have been identified as probably belonging to a hitherto unknown race of the greater dwarf shrew. Whereas the skull length of the three known South African *Suncus* species varies from 14 to 17 millimetres, the measurements of intact skulls of the Kruger Park form are 20 and 21 millimetres in length, *i.e.* they are appreciably larger than those of any of the known races of the biggest of the three, the greater dwarf shrew, *Suncus lixus*. Unfortunately, despite extensive collecting, no live specimens have as yet come to hand, and a description of this animal, the distribution of which seems to cover most of the Park, will have to remain in abeyance until trapping operations are successful.

ORDER INSECTIVORA

Family Erinaceidae

Hedgehogs

Southern African hedgehog

Atelerix frontalis

Suider-Afrikaanse krimpvarkie

Distribution: The hedgehog is very localised and is only known from two sight records in the higher-lying grassveld areas around Pretoriuskop at Mlangeni and Kambeni.

Habitat: Grassland and bush savanna.

Habits: The hedgehog appears to hibernate during the cold, drier months of May to September, but is found abroad with the onset of the rains in October. It occurs solitarily or in pairs, and is largely nocturnal. When it is walking, its legs appear abnormally long for the size of its body. The hedgehog lies up during the day in piles of debris, in thick underbrush or grass, in holes or among rocks. The only occasion when permanent nest-sites are used is when females are nursing a litter. Otherwise individuals find day-time refuges wherever they are. When alarmed, the hedgehog rolls up in a tight ball, the spines erected to point outwards. It utters a soft growl on occasion. It is preyed upon by such predators as eagle-owls and hyaenas.

Diet: The hedgehog is omnivorous, feeding on insects, millipedes, termites, earthworms, slugs, frogs, young birds, small mice, eggs, wild fruits and vegetable matter.

Breeding: The young are born during the warm, wet summer months from October to March. Nests are constructed under debris, piles of grass, roots or stones. The disused nests of rodents may also be utilised. The young are born with their eyes closed. The gestation period is about 40 days and the litter size ranges from three to six.

Southern African hedgehog

ORDER
INSECTIVORA

Family
Chrysochloridae

Golden moles

Yellow golden mole

Calcochloris obtusirostris

Geelgouemol

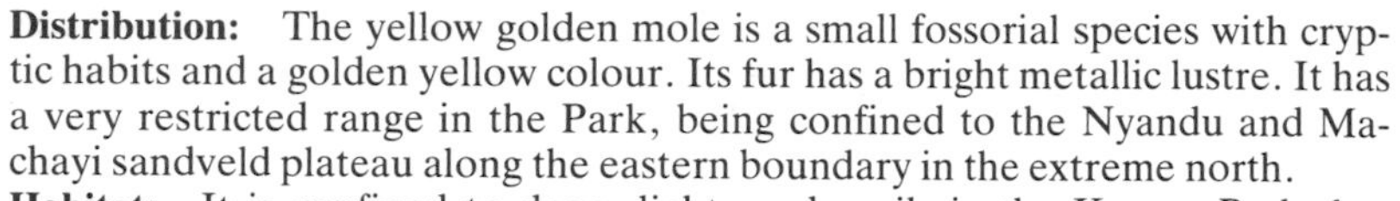

Distribution: The yellow golden mole is a small fossorial species with cryptic habits and a golden yellow colour. Its fur has a bright metallic lustre. It has a very restricted range in the Park, being confined to the Nyandu and Machayi sandveld plateau along the eastern boundary in the extreme north.
Habitat: It is confined to deep, light sandy soils in the Kruger Park, but elsewhere within its known range of distribution it also inhabits coastal sands and riparian sandy alluvium.
Habits: This fossorial species constructs elevated, temporary, subsurface burrows which are a typical feature of the sandy regions which it inhabits. It also, however, appears to excavate a modest but permanent underground tunnel system amongst the roots of bushes or grass tussocks. From here an individual will meander in search of food, "swimming" in the sand just under the surface, thus creating the typical impermanent subsurface tunnels. It is very rarely encountered outside its subterranean burrows and is relatively difficult to capture. However, it has been noticed that heavy rain will force some individuals to the surface for short periods. It is preyed upon by the long-tailed garter snake, *Elapsoidea sundevallii*.
Diet: It is particularly partial to tenebrionid beetle larvae and harvester termites, but it will also take the young and even adults of burrowing lizards such as *Typhlosaurus* and *Zygaspis*.
Breeding: No records to date.

Yellow
golden mole

Juliana's golden mole *Amblysomus julianae*

Juliana-gouemol

Distribution: In the Park the distribution of this rare species is confined to the sandy, granitic soils north and south of the Pretoriuskop/Numbi road. Southwards its range extends to the Matjulwana Valley and northwards to the foothills of Numbi Kop. The first specimens of this relatively recently described species were collected in the Mavukani and Fayi/Sithungwane areas of the Kruger National Park during November 1960. Additional material was obtained near Numbi Gate and north of the Matjulwana Picket.

Habits: No information is available from the wild, but a live specimen has been kept in a vivarium with clayey soil, unlike the sandy soil in which it was collected. It spent most of its time underground, coming to the surface only when it was hungry. It also appeared to prefer moist soil, presumably because tunnels are easier to construct and more durable under such conditions. It is noticeable that the characteristic elevated and meandering subsurface tunnels of this animal are more commonly encountered after rains than during dry spells. Above ground it is sensitive to vibration, but apparently not to sound or light. When agitated it may emit a squeaking noise. It is active both by day and night, although perhaps more so at night.

Diet: A live specimen was maintained in the Transvaal Museum on a diet of ground beef, augmented from time to time with live earthworms, cockroaches, meal-worm larvae, grasshoppers and other insects, but did not appear to eat snails or slugs. It sometimes ate its food where encountered, but more often carried it into its burrow. Food items were held in the forepaws when eating.

Breeding: A specimen collected in February was pregnant, with one foetus.

ORDER
CHIROPTERA

SUBORDER
MEGACHIROPTERA

Family
Pteropodidae

Fruit bats

Wahlberg's epauletted fruit bat

Wahlberg's epauletted fruit bat *Epomophorus wahlbergi*

Wahlberg-witkolvrugtevlermuis

Distribution: So far, this species has only been recorded from Pretoriuskop and Malelane in the southern region and from Punda Maria and Pafuri in the far northern region of the Park, although it undoubtedly also frequents suitable habitats elsewhere.
Habitat: Savannas, tropical and riparian forests as well as thickets where there are fruit-bearing trees.
Habits: Wahlberg's epauletted fruit bat is a larger species and of stouter build than the closely related Peters's epauletted fruit bat. Colonies roost during the daylight hours in the canopy of trees in the shade of thick foliage, sometimes in considerable numbers and often in association with Peters's epauletted fruit bats. Roosting individuals are constantly on the alert against predators. They exhibit considerable local movement in search of food, although a specific roosting-site is regularly used while the bats are temporarily resident in a particular area. Their nightly activity is at its peak during the early evening when they concentrate on feeding; this is followed by social interaction and sporadic feeding during the rest of the night. Large numbers may congregate to feed in trees bearing an abundance of ripe fruit, wild figtrees for example being especially favoured. Quite often a fruit is picked and carried to an adjacent tree where it can be consumed without the interference of other bats. Typically these fruit bats take a few bites from a fruit, then drop it and depart in search of another. The digestion of fruit meals is exceptionally rapid.

Diet: Mainly fruit, such as sycamore-figs, jackal-berry and moepel, but judging from the remnants of beetles and other insects in the stomach contents of some specimens examined, they are occasionally partly insectivorous.
Breeding: Females give birth to a single offspring from the latter half of November till about the end of December.

Peters's epauletted fruit bat *Epomophorus crypturus*

Peters-witkolvrugtevlermuis

Distribution: Peters's epauletted fruit bat has been recorded from suitable localities throughout the entire area of the Park.
Habitat: Savannas and especially riparian forests where there are fruit-bearing trees.
Habits: This is a nomadic species often attracted in great numbers to riparian and other forested areas in the Park by ripening wild or cultivated fruits during the wet season, particularly those of figs and the jackal-berry and nyala trees. The monotonous bell-like calls of the males are then an integral part of the nocturnal symphony in these areas. The newly born young are carried attached to the nipple when the mothers forage. In general, Peters's epauletted fruit bat is very similar to Wahlberg's epauletted fruit bat in behaviour.
Diet: They feed mainly on the fruits of wild and cultivated trees and they can become a menace in mango and litchi orchards in the lowveld.
Breeding: Single young attached to their mothers have been commonly recorded in December and January, suggesting a birth peak during the latter half of November and December.

Peters's epauletted fruit bat

Egyptian fruit bat

Rousettus aegyptiacus

Egiptiese vrugtevlermuis

Distribution: A smaller species than the epauletted fruit bats, the Egyptian fruit bat has only recently been recorded in the extreme northern area of the Park along the Luvuvhu and Limpopo rivers at Pafuri. One colony numbering several thousands utilises a cave at Lanner Gorge as a day-time refuge; there may be others. In the rest of the Transvaal it is also rare and has only been recorded at four localities in the eastern lowveld. There is also a record from Chikwarakwara on the Limpopo in south-eastern Zimbabwe.
Habitat: The species exhibits a wide habitat tolerance, occurring both in tropical forests and savannas. Individuals emerge from their cave at dusk, and can cover distances of up to 30 kilometres in search of food. During summer they forage up and down the Luvuvhu riverine forests for fruit, mostly in sycamore-fig trees. During winter, however, these animals are under stress for food and have been found in remote areas of dry savanna, presumably searching for more scattered food sources.
Habits: Unlike the other fruit-eating bats, which use trees for day-time roosts, Egyptian fruit bats are partial to caves, where they often congregate in large numbers. During the day, roosting colonies are characterised by restlessness and constant noisy squabbles amongst individuals. From these caves they range widely in search of food. Their distribution is correlated with the presence of suitable caves as resting-places as well as the year-round availability of fruit. It is apparently the only frugivorous (fruit-eating) bat species which can navigate by means of echolocation – enabling it to utilise the dark interior of caves. This attribute probably also explains its remarkable power of manoeuvring. When foraging, females carry their offspring with them, the

infants clinging to their bellies and biting on to a nipple. Instances where such young weigh as much as a third of the mother's mass have been recorded.
Diet: Wild fruit such as sycamore-figs constitute the main food source for these bats, but in the Transvaal they have been found to be very partial to litchis. Where such are available they will also feed on dates, guavas, mangoes and bananas. The bats pick the fruit while hovering and then carry it away to a nearby tree where they feed while hanging suspended from a branch by their hindfeet. Like other fruit bats they are wasteful feeders and only take one or two bites from the fruit before it is discarded.
Breeding: Mating takes place during June, and a single young is born to each female during late November or early December.

ORDER
CHIROPTERA

SUBORDER
MICROCHIROPTERA

Family
Emballonuridae

Tomb bats

Mauritian tomb bat

Taphozous mauritianus

Witlyfvlermuis

Distribution: This species is apparently rare in the Park, but has been recorded singly, in pairs, or most often in small groups, at localities throughout the entire area.
Habitat: Although essentially an open woodland savanna species, the Mauritian tomb bat is, however, also found in clearings in tropical forest.
Habits: They rest during daylight hours clinging upside-down to tree-trunks, rock-faces or on the outside of the walls or under the eaves of houses. When approached they quickly move sideways in a stealthy, crab-like manner to hide in crevices or out of sight on the other side of the tree-trunk or wall. Pairs or small numbers may roost together, but the Mauritian tomb bat is never highly gregarious. This species has large eyes, and presumably possesses good sight.
Diet: It may on rare occasions feed during daylight hours as it has been observed taking butterflies and other insects on the wing. It is, however, essentially nocturnal. No detailed list of food items is available.
Breeding: Young have been observed clinging to their mothers during October whereas a number of females, each carrying a single foetus, were collected during February in Zimbabwe.

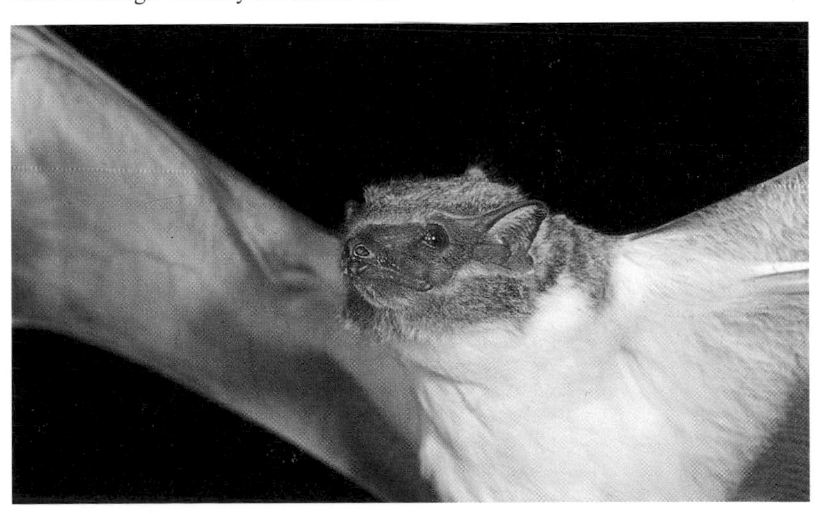

Mauritian tomb bat

ORDER
CHIROPTERA

SUBORDER
MICROCHIROPTERA

Family
Nycteridae

Slit-faced bats

Wood's slit-faced bat

Nycteris woodi

Wood-spleetneusvlermuis

Distribution: Wood's slit-faced bat was until recently known only from eastern Zambia and south-eastern Zimbabwe. A taxonomic revision of the genus, however, then showed that some specimens acquired from the Pafuri area and formerly believed to be *N. thebaica*, were incorrectly identified and are in fact *N. woodi.* This species has since been found to be relatively common in the extreme northern regions of the Kruger National Park.
Habitat: Although it is essentially a savanna woodland species, individuals are often observed feeding in riparian forests at night. Slit-faced bats are very sensitive to low humidity and high temperatures and their survival thus depends on the availability of day-time roosts which offer a suitably stable environment, such as caves and hollow baobab trees.
Habits: By day, colonies of loosely spaced individuals ranging from a few to several hundred individuals use caves, hollow baobab trees and old buildings as day-time roosts. Wood's slit-faced bat is, like other nycterid bats, a slow but very agile flier possessing extremely sensitive echolocating abilities which allow it to detect and glean insect prey even when the latter is resting on leaves, branches or the ground. Since it is not dependent on flying insects as a source of food it can remain feeding actively throughout the night, even after the early-evening abundance of aerial insects has declined. Small groups congregate in sheltered night-roosts after an initial early-evening feeding bout, from where individuals range on short feeding forays throughout the remainder of the night.
Diet: Small soft-bodied insects.
Breeding: Females give birth to single offspring during the latter half of November.

Wood's slit-faced bat, with newly born offspring, roosting in the attic of a deserted building.

Egyptian slit-faced bat

Hildebrandt's horseshoe bat. This individual has been fitted with bands on the forearm to facilitate individual identification, as well as with a miniature radio-transmitter to allow scientists to study its movements and behaviour.

Egyptian slit-faced bat *Nycteris thebaica*

Egiptiese spleetneusvlermuis

Distribution: This is one of the more common bat species, and it is distributed throughout the entire area of the Park.
Habitat and habits: This bat is a savanna species with a wide habitat tolerance. During the day, colonies roost in large numbers in caves, under the roofs of houses, in hollow tree-trunks or in disused huts. Following an initial bout of intensive feeding shortly after dark, individuals congregate in a night-roost where they rest, groom and interact socially. When larger insect prey is captured the bats return to their hunting-roosts to devour it.
Breeding: Gravid females with single foetuses have been recorded during August and October and lactating females during November.

ORDER CHIROPTERA

SUBORDER MICROCHIROPTERA

Family Rhinolophidae

Horseshoe bats

Hildebrandt's horseshoe bat *Rhinolophus hildebrandtii*

Hildebrandt-saalneusvlermuis

Distribution: Hildebrandt's horseshoe bat is found in certain caves, disused buildings and hollow baobab trees in the northern half of the Park.
Habitat: It is a savanna woodland species, whose local occurrence appears to be determined by the availability of day-time roosts in the form of caves, hollow baobab trees, old buildings or culverts. Day-time roosts are characterised by a high relative humidity and a constant temperature lower than the day-time ambient temperatures. It appears to prefer hunting amongst dense

bush, a preference which is facilitated by the remarkable flight agility and acute echolocation abilities characteristic of all horseshoe bats.
Habits: Hildebrandt's horseshoe bat is encountered singly, in pairs or more often in colonies of up to several scores of individuals. It is sometimes associated with other cave-dwelling species such as Sundevall's leaf-nosed bat and Schreibers's long-fingered bat. During day-time, individuals hang in loose aggregations suspended by their hindfeet from the ceiling of the roost. The wings are neatly folded around the body, rather like a cloak. At dusk, Hildebrandt's horseshoe bats emerge and disperse for a period of up to two hours of intensive solitary feeding on the wing. Thereafter they seek out night-roosts in the form of branches in open clearings, where they groom and also continue to hunt rather in the manner of a flycatcher, *i.e.* darting out to catch an insect whereupon they return to the perch to consume it at leisure.
Diet: Medium-sized moths and beetles.
Breeding: Females give birth to a single young during the latter half of November or in December. Young are left behind in the day-time roost while the mothers hunt for prey during the night.

Rüppell's horseshoe bat *Rhinolophus fumigatus*

Rüppell-saalneusvlermuis

Distribution: This is a species with a wide distribution, ranging from the Cape Province north to East Africa; in the Park, however, it is known only from specimens collected in a hollow baobab tree in the Mashicindzudzi firebreak, in the Olifants River Gorge and at several localities near Pafuri in the north.
Habitat and habits: It is a savanna species which roosts during the day in caves or crevices in rocks as well as in culverts and hollow trees, usually in small numbers. As far as can be ascertained, it is very similar to Hildebrandt's horseshoe bat in its habitat preferences and behaviour.
Diet: Rüppell's horseshoe bat feeds on a variety of medium-sized soft-bodied insects, including moths and beetles.
Breeding: Females give birth to single offspring annually, with the birth peak towards the end of November and beginning of December.

Rüppell's horseshoe bat

Geoffroy's horseshoe bat

Darling's horseshoe bat

Geoffroy's horseshoe bat *Rhinolophus clivosus*

Geoffroy-saalneusvlermuis

Distribution: This is another horseshoe bat with a wide geographical range, but which in the Park appears to be rare; so far it has only been recorded at Punda Maria Rest Camp and at Pafuri in the north, with a single record from Skukuza. It is very likely that this species has been overlooked elsewhere in the Park.
Habitat and habits: It is a savanna species that rests during the day in caves, under the roofs of houses, in lofts and in other dark and humid places.
Diet: Moths and small beetles have been recorded.
Breeding: Pregnant females, each carrying a single near-term foetus, have been collected during November.

Darling's horseshoe bat *Rhinolophus darlingi*

Darling-saalneusvlermuis

Distribution: Darling's horseshoe bat is widespread throughout the Park. It is a gregarious species, congregating in large numbers by day in certain caves, amongst piles of loose boulders or under the floors of disused houses.
Habitat and habits: A savanna species, Darling's horseshoe bat has been found to share its chosen roosts with other cave-dwelling species such as the Egyptian slit-faced bat and Schreibers's long-fingered bat.
Diet: Insectivorous.
Breeding: A pregnant female with a single foetus has been collected in October.

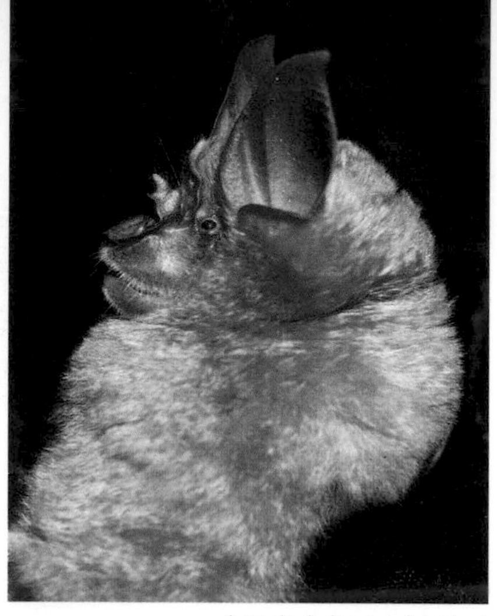

Lander's horseshoe bat

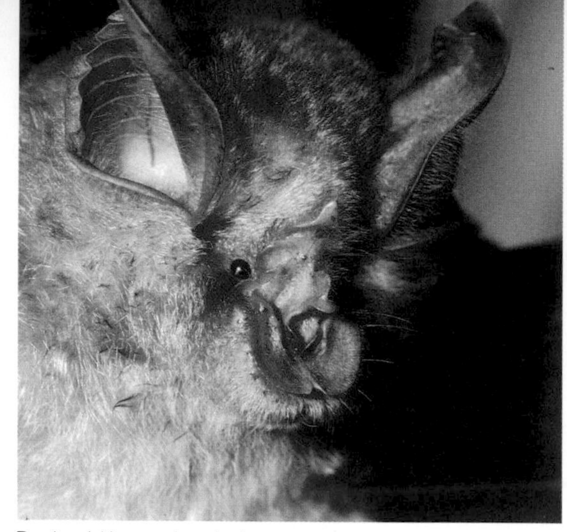

Bushveld horseshoe bat

Lander's horseshoe bat

Rhinolophus landeri

Lander-saalneusvlermuis

Distribution: Lander's horseshoe bat has been recorded from a cave near Ngirivani, from an outbuilding at the W.N.L.A. quarters at Pafuri (a fairly large community) and from Shirhombe Picket.
Habitat and habits: Like Darling's horseshoe bat, this is also a savanna species, roosting during the day in caves and under roofs. Several colour phases of the fur have been recorded, ranging from dull grey to bright orange. Specimens of the latter form are very conspicuous in flight.
Diet: Insectivorous, particularly favouring small soft-bodied insects like moths.
Breeding: No information is available.

Bushveld horseshoe bat

Rhinolophus simulator

Bosveld-saalneusvlermuis

Distribution: The bushveld horseshoe bat has always been expected to occur in the Park because of its widespread occurrence in the Transvaal, Mozambique, Zimbabwe and further north in Africa, but until recently solid proof has been lacking. Its presence has now been confirmed from the central districts of the Park as well as from Pafuri.
Habitat: It is a savanna woodland species. Like all horseshoe bat species, the bushveld horseshoe bat requires the cool and humid environment of caves, hollow baobab trees and old buildings for day-time refuges.
Habits: Individuals, loosely arranged in small clusters, spend the days suspended from the ceilings of their day-roosts, out of reach of predators. The bushveld horseshoe bat is a slow but very acrobatic flier, a technique which allows it to hunt for prey amongst vegetation and close to the ground. Following an initial spurt of early-evening hunting activity, individuals continue to hunt sporadically throughout the night in the manner of a flycatcher.
Diet: A variety of small soft-bodied insects are preyed upon.
Breeding: Females give birth to single offspring during late November.

Swinny's horseshoe bat

Rhinolophus swinnyi

Swinny-saalneusvlermuis

Distribution: The occurrence of this species in the Park was confirmed during 1982 from the Pafuri region in the north-eastern corner of the Park, where it has since been irregularly encountered. Although these are to date the only known records of occurrence of this species from the Transvaal, it is nevertheless believed to be a permanent resident of the entire eastern Transvaal Lowveld where it has presumably simply been overlooked.
Habitat: By day small colonies utilise the cool, humid interiors of caves, crevices, hollow trees, culverts and old buildings as refuges. By night this species frequents a variety of well-wooded habitats in search of prey.
Habits: Individuals hunt solitarily, generally close to the ground. An early-evening period of continuous hunting is followed by periods of rest and grooming in sheltered night-roosts, alternating with short feeding bouts.
Diet: A variety of small soft-bodied insects are taken.
Breeding: Females give birth seasonally, with a single offspring born to each female during early summer.

Swinny's horseshoe bat

ORDER
CHIROPTERA

SUBORDER
MICROCHIROPTERA

Family
Hipposideridae

Leaf-nosed bats

Commerson's leaf-nosed bat

Hipposideros commersoni

Commerson-bladneusvlermuis

Distribution: This is one of the largest insectivorous bats in Africa, with adults attaining a body mass of up to 150 grams. It has recently been recorded for the first time within the Republic from Pafuri in the north-eastern regions of the Park. Since its initial discovery at Pafuri, adults as well as subadults have been sporadically encountered, which suggests that it is rare, yet at least a seasonally permanent resident of the Park.
Habitat and habits: Over most of its range it is associated with savanna woodland, although it is also found in high forests. At Pafuri it has so far only been encountered in riverine forests. During the day colonies of up to several hundreds roost in caves. From observations made on colonies in Botswana and South West Africa/Namibia, it is evidently a seasonally migrating species, returning to the same caves each season.
Diet: Feeds mostly on large beetles caught on the wing.
Breeding: A female caught at Pafuri during October carried a single foetus.

Commerson's
leaf-nosed bat

Sundevall's leaf-nosed bat

Hipposideros caffer

Sundevall-bladneusvlermuis

Distribution: An inhabitant of the drier, open savannas, Sundevall's leaf-nosed bat has been recorded throughout the entire area of the Park.
Habitat: It occurs widely throughout most of sub-Saharan Africa in savanna woodlands. Analyses of records of occurrence suggest that the availability of surface water and associated riparian vegetation as well as suitable day-time refuges are essential habitat requirements for this bat.
Habits: This is a communal species often encountered in large numbers in its chosen roosts (caves, rock crevices or under the roofs of disused buildings). One particular community at Munywini has been known to inhabit the same cave for twenty years. Several different colour phases are found. The bright orange phase is most spectacular when the animal is disturbed and flits through sunlit areas in or around the day-roost. It has been suggested that the orange colour phase is actually caused by the staining effect of high ammoniac concentrations emanating from accumulated guano. After an initial bout

Sundevall's leaf-nosed bat

of solitary intensive feeding, individuals converge on a night-roost within the feeding area where they groom and engage in social interaction, and whence they depart on irregular short feeding sorties throughout the night. Individuals hunt for prey amongst dense vegetation, indicating that they possess very sophisticated echolocating and manoeuvring abilities. Casual observations on a number of colonies suggest this species to be a seasonal migrator.

Diet. Small, soft-bodied insects.

Breeding: Gravid females have been recorded from August to October. A single offspring is born to each female.

The short-eared trident bat, *Cloeotis percivali*, has been collected at Komatipoort near the southern boundary of the Kruger National Park, but this cave-dwelling species has not as yet been recorded within the boundaries of the Park.

ORDER CHIROPTERA

SUBORDER MICROCHIROPTERA

Family Vespertilionidae

Common bats

Schreibers's long-fingered bat *Miniopterus schreibersii*

Schreibers-grotvlermuis

Distribution: A common species, Schreibers's long-fingered bat is widely distributed in suitable habitats throughout the Park.
Habitat: These bats appear to have a wide habitat tolerance, being found in both arid and well-watered country, on the fringes of tropical forest, in woodlands, in open coastal scrub thickets as well as in highveld grasslands.
Habits: Schreibers's long-fingered bat is a communal and seasonally migratory species normally associated with caves where it roosts during the daylight hours, often in very large colonies numbering several hundreds of thousands. It has also been taken under the roofs of houses, in mine-shafts and in adits. Colonies roost against the ceilings and walls of their day-time refuges, packed closely together. This species has been found to migrate annually to cold and moist caves where it hibernates during the winter months. In summer it migrates back to woodland areas with abundant food resources, where its young are born and raised. Newly born long-fingered bats are deposited in nursery colonies in maternity caves where the mothers visit them and attend to their needs. Mating takes place during late summer following the migration to hibernation caves.
Diet: Insectivorous.
Breeding: Females with well-developed single foetuses have been collected in October. Apparently mating takes place during autumn in hibernation caves while parturition occurs during early summer in maternity caves.

Welwitsch's hairy bat *Myotis welwitschii*

Welwitsch-langhaarvlermuis

Distribution: This rare and strikingly coloured bat has been recorded from a few isolated localities in the south and from Matukwala Dam and the W.N.L.A. garden in the north of the Park.
Habitat and habits: Welwitsch's hairy bat is a savanna woodland species. Solitary specimens have been taken in trees or low bushes but little is known about the social habits, diet or breeding of this species.

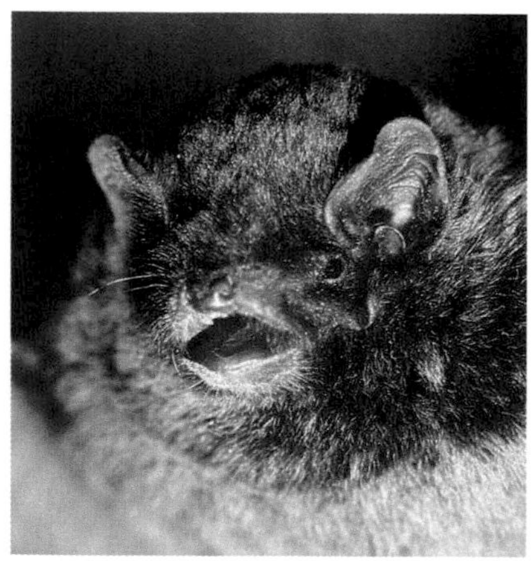

Schreibers's long-fingered bat

Welwitsch's hairy bat

Temminck's hairy bat

Rufous hairy bat

Temminck's hairy bat

Myotis tricolor

Temminck-langhaarvlermuis

Distribution: Temminck's hairy bat is apparently not common in the Park, and only a few specimens have been collected at Satara and more recently at Pafuri in the far northern region. The species is nowhere common throughout its wide geographical range from the Cape to Ethiopia.

Habitat and habits: The specimens on record from the Park were collected on the wing with dust-shot or by netting, and consequently no information is available from this area regarding its preferred resting-places. Elsewhere, however, it has been observed to have a preference for wet caves and disused mine-shafts. Seasonal migration has been recorded, but the exact details of this are still unknown. It is a communal species, but nothing is known of its feeding habits.

Breeding: No information is available from the Park. In the Cape the birth season has been recorded to extend from late October to the middle of November.

Rufous hairy bat

Myotis bocagei

Rooi langhaarvlermuis

Distribution: A series of specimens representing this rare species was recently collected in the W.N.L.A. garden at Pafuri, near the confluence of the Luvuvhu and Limpopo rivers. Subsequently this bat has been found at several localities along the Luvuvhu. A single record of the rufous hairy bat exists from immediately south of Vila Gouveia in Mozambique. The Pafuri specimens represent the first records of this species within the borders of the Republic of South Africa. A further specimen was recently taken at Skukuza, which represents a 300-kilometre southward extension of its known distribution range.

Habitat and habits: Very little is known about the habitat preferences and habits of this species. The rufous hairy bat appears to have a predilection for forests, although it has also been recorded in woodland savannas near permanent surface water. In West Africa solitary individuals have been found to take refuge during daylight hours in banana plants, but no information is available from the Kruger Park records since the specimens were all netted.

Diet: Insectivorous.

Breeding: Unknown.

Rüppell's pipistrelle

Pipistrellus rueppellii

Rüppell-vlermuis

Distribution: Although Rüppell's pipistrelle is widespread in tropical Africa, it has only recently been discovered south of the Limpopo River, from the Pafuri region in the Kruger National Park, where it is now regularly encountered. These are still the only records from within the borders of the Republic.
Habitat and habits: Throughout its range this species is associated with riverine forests. At Pafuri it is invariably encountered in this habitat. Very little is known of its biology, although it has been observed at Pafuri to be active only during the early evening.
Diet: It preys on small insects which are caught on the wing.
Breeding: Females carrying single foetuses have been recorded during September, October and early November, suggesting a birth season during the latter half of November and early December.

Rüppell's pipistrelle

Kuhl's pipistrelle

Pipistrellus kuhlii

Kuhl-vlermuis

Distribution: Kuhl's pipistrelle is known only from a single locality in the Park, *viz.* Skukuza. It has also been collected at Hectorspruit, just south of the Crocodile River boundary of the Park, and at Phalaborwa near the western boundary of the Park.
Habitat: Kuhl's pipistrelle has a wide habitat tolerance, but records from elsewhere in the Southern African Subregion suggest an association with well-watered terrain. This species takes refuge by day under the loose bark of dead trees. In Zimbabwe it has also been found resting in rock crevices.
Habits: It is a gregarious species, occurring in small colonies of up to 12 individuals huddled closely together. Kuhl's pipistrelle is one of the first bat species to emerge at dusk. It is a slow but very acrobatic flier, hunting small insects wherever they occur in quantity. It is often seen flying with other bats, over open, still water surfaces.
Diet: Insectivorous.
Breeding: Pregnant females, each with a single foetus, have been collected in October.

Kuhl's pipistrelle

Anchieta's pipistrelle

Pipistrellus anchietai

Anchieta-vlermuis

Distribution: A single specimen of this species was netted near the reservoir at Skukuza. Despite all efforts, no further specimens have as yet been procured.

Habitat and habits. Elsewhere through its range Anchieta's pipistrelle is associated with woodland savanna but very little is known about its habits.

Diet: Small insects, which are caught on the wing during the early part of the evening.

Breeding: No information.

Anchieta's pipistrelle

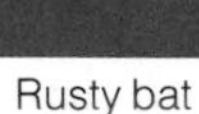

Rusty bat

Banana bat

Rusty bat

Pipistrellus rusticus

Roeskleurvlermuis

Distribution: The rusty bat is known from only a few localities in the Punda Maria and Pafuri areas of the Park. It has also been collected at Pretoria, Hectorspruit and Tzaneen in the Transvaal and at the Shashi/Limpopo river confluence in Zimbabwe. Where it occurs in the Kruger Park it is a particularly common bat.
Habitat: All records in the Southern African Subregion are from dry savanna country, but always in close proximity to permanent surface water with its associated vegetation.
Habits: Very little is known about the habits of this bat. It has been stated that it is a slow flier which prefers hunting its prey over water or in riverine forests. It may take refuge during the day under the loose bark of trees. Observations at Pafuri indicate that it hunts actively during the first hour immediately after sunset, whereas it is seldom (if ever) observed later at night.
Diet: Insectivorous.
Breeding: Pregnant females were collected during September, October and November, while lactating females were recorded during December. The males have grossly enlarged testes during early winter, suggesting that they mate at this time and that there is delayed embryonic development during winter.

Banana bat

Pipistrellus nanus

Piesangvlermuis

Distribution: Although the banana bat is a common and widespread species in surrounding territories, in the Park it has only been collected at Skukuza, Pretoriuskop and Malelane in the Southern District, Satara in the Central District and at Pafuri in the far north.
Habitat and Habits: As the name implies, these little bats are almost exclusively found where bananas and plantains are grown, or where there are groves of wild bananas, and are therefore not found in arid and semi-arid

areas. During the day they rest in the rolled-up terminal leaves of banana or plantain trees, often packed together in large numbers; alternatively they may be found in the bunches of fruit, where they hide close to the central stem. They have also been recorded from oil palms and occasionally from under the thatch of huts. Apart from the fact that they are insectivorous, little else is known about these petite bats.
Breeding: Pregnant females, the great majority carrying two foetuses, were recorded during September and October.

Butterfly bat

Chalinolobus variegatus

Vlindervlermuis

Distribution: Specimens of this rare bat with its characteristic variegated wing membranes are collected at irregular intervals in the vegetable garden of the W.N.L.A. at Pafuri as well as at various other spots along the Luvuvhu River. The butterfly bat is sparsely distributed throughout its African range and uncommon in most collections. The Kruger Park specimens represent only the second record of its occurrence within the borders of the Transvaal. Roberts collected the species from the Soutpansberg around 1935. This species was previously known as *Glauconycteris variegata* but most authorities now agree that there is no justification for separating the African genus *Glauconycteris* from the allied Australasian genus *Chalinolobus*.
Habitat and habits: From the limited records available from other parts of Africa it appears to be a savanna species, although all the Park records are from riverine forests. It is likely that they rest in trees during the day and that they are not communal. The original Kruger Park specimen was one of a group of three captured in an orchard of litchi trees while suspended in a dense cluster of leaves. On three occasions two individuals were netted while flying in close formation, something so far never observed in any other species. The significance of this observation is as yet unknown.
Diet: Insectivorous.
Breeding: No information is available.

Butterfly bat

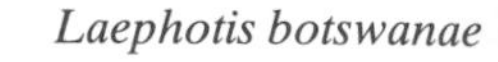

Botswana long-eared bat *Laephotis botswanae*

Botswana-langoorvlermuis

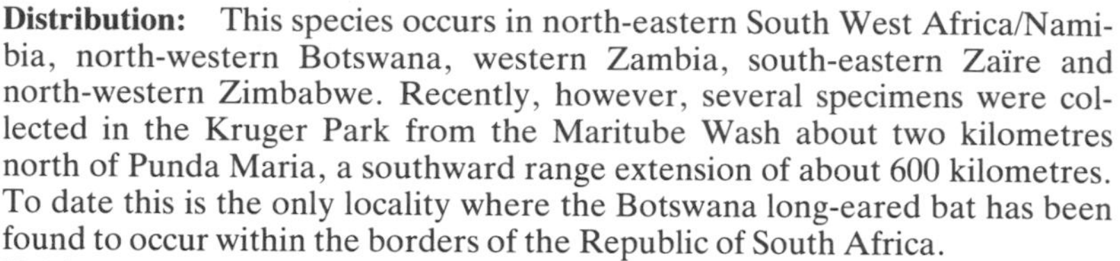

Distribution: This species occurs in north-eastern South West Africa/Namibia, north-western Botswana, western Zambia, south-eastern Zaïre and north-western Zimbabwe. Recently, however, several specimens were collected in the Kruger Park from the Maritube Wash about two kilometres north of Punda Maria, a southward range extension of about 600 kilometres. To date this is the only locality where the Botswana long-eared bat has been found to occur within the borders of the Republic of South Africa.
Habitat and habits: All existing records for the Botswana long-eared bat are from dry woodland savanna, but always in the vicinity of permanent surface water. During the day individuals take refuge in rock crevices and under the loose bark of trees. Little else is known about the biology of this species.
Diet: A variety of small soft-bodied insects.
Breeding: No information is available.

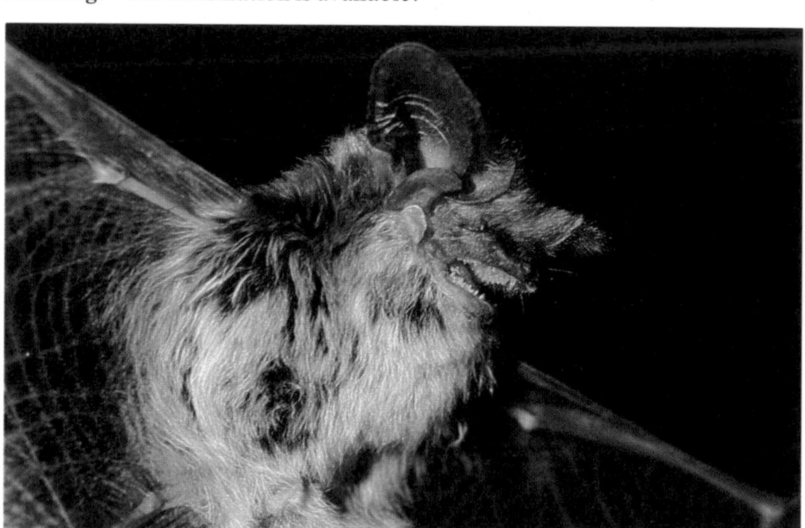

Botswana long-eared bat

Long-tailed serotine bat *Eptesicus hottentotus*

Langstertdakvlermuis

Distribution: The long-tailed serotine bat is known from scattered localities in two disjunct areas in southern Africa, *viz.* Zimbabwe and adjacent countries on the one hand and the Cape and South West Africa/Namibia on the other. It appears to be uncommon everywhere. Recently, however, it was found to occur in the gap between these two distributional areas, at Pafuri in the north-eastern corner of the Kruger National Park. So far this is the only locality from which this species has been recorded in the Transvaal.
Habitat and habits: From what little information is available, it appears that the long-tailed serotine bat is either associated with broken or mountainous country, or as in the case of the Pafuri population, with riverine forests. It has been found to use caves, buildings and rock crevices as day-time roosts.
Diet: Insectivorous.
Breeding: No information is available.

Long-tailed serotine bat

Melck's serotine bat

Eptesicus melckorum

Melck-dakvlermuis

Distribution: The presence of this species at Skukuza as well as at several localities in the Pafuri district of the Kruger National Park became known only recently. Since it is a relatively common bat elsewhere, it has probably simply been overlooked in other parts of the Park. Some taxonomic inconsistencies relating to the specimens from the Park remain to be clarified; for the time being, however, they have been assigned to *E. melckorum*.
Habitat and habits: Little is known about the biology of this species but it appears to be associated with wooded areas of semi-arid regions as well as with dry woodland savannas.
Diet: It feeds on a variety of aerial insects during the early evening.
Breeding: Lactating females have been netted during December.

Melck's serotine bat

Cape serotine bat with two recently born young attached to her nipples, in which manner they are transported for the first few days following birth.

Cape serotine bat

Eptesicus capensis

Kaapse dakvlermuis

Distribution: The Cape serotine bat, which has a wide distribution in Africa south of the Sahara, is relatively rare in the Kruger National Park, although available records indicate an even distribution throughout.
Habitat and habits: Apparently it is a species with a wide habitat tolerance, occurring in semi-desert as well as high rainfall areas. Cape serotine bats rest during the day, singly or in small groups, in the roofs of houses or under the loose bark of trees. They appear to engage in a short intensive bout of feeding shortly after sunset, whereafter such activity virtually ceases for the rest of the night.
Diet: Small soft-bodied insects, including mosquitoes.
Breeding: Pregnant females with one to three foetuses have been collected in October and November, and lactating females have been taken in December.

Aloe bat

Aloe bat

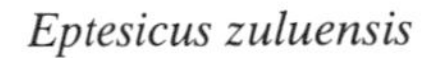

Eptesicus zuluensis

Aalwynvlermuis

Distribution: This relatively rare serotine bat, which was described as recently as 1924, is known in the Park from only a few localities in the northern district, *viz.* Stangene Windmill, Shashanga and Pafuri along the Luvuvhu River. Based on the evidence of genetic studies, in this field guide we regard it as separate from the closely related *E. somalicus*.
Habitat and habits: The aloe bat is a savanna species which apparently favours the clusters of dry leaves around the stems of tree aloes such as *A. marlothii* as resting-places during the day. From these roosts they emerge at dusk to flit about in search of food in open glades between the trees. Kruger Park specimens have all been collected in the vicinity of open water.
Breeding: No records are available.

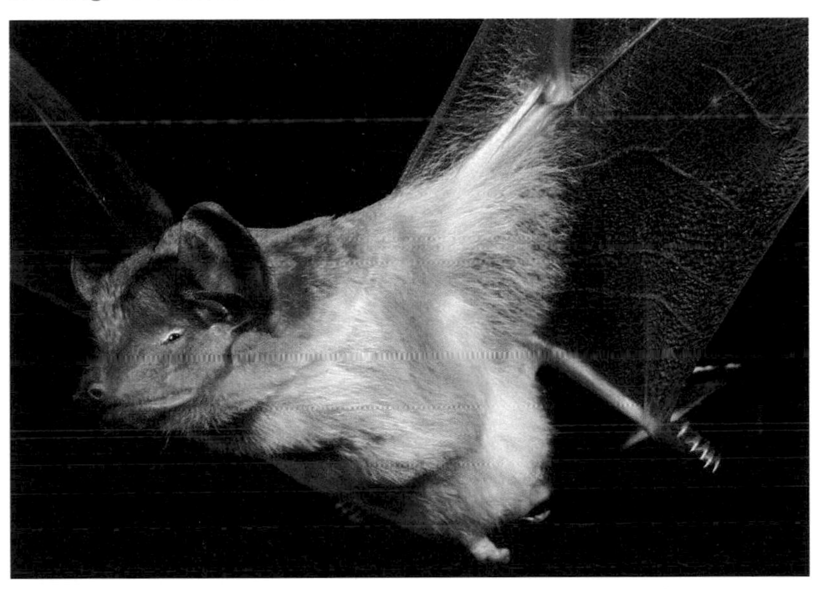

Yellow house bat

Yellow house bat

Scotophilus dinganii

Geel dakvlermuis

Distribution: The yellow house bat is generally distributed throughout the Park but is relatively uncommon except in the Punda Maria/Pafuri area where it is exceedingly common.
Habitat and habits: It has a wide habitat tolerance, but is more common in savannas and rare in semi-desert areas. During the day it rests in hollow trees or in the roofs of houses where it crawls into narrow crevices. It often enters houses at night. They roost solitarily or in small groups. Yellow house bats are particularly efficient feeders, specimens collected shortly after sunset invariably having their stomachs distended with insects. It is presumed therefore that they are active for only a short period after sundown, and in fact they are very seldom encountered later at night. They appear to use the same general hunting area throughout the year, although they are noticeably less active during winter when insects are in short supply.

Breeding: Gravid females have been collected in Zimbabwe and at Pafuri from October to the beginning of November, whereas lactating females have been recorded during the latter half of November and December. The normal number of foetuses per female is two, although triplets have been recorded.

Lesser yellow house bat *Scotophilus borbonicus*

Klein geel dakvlermuis

Distribution: The lesser yellow house bat is considerably smaller than the yellow house bat and has duller yellow fur on the belly. In the Park it has been collected at Skukuza, at Nsemani Windmill, as well as near Satara and at the Phalaborwa Gate, and at a few localities in the far northern sector of the Park where it is common. It appears to be one of the more widespread and common bat species of the Park.
Habitat: Its range of distribution is closely correlated with savanna areas, particularly stands of tall mopane. Hollows in tall mopane trees are favoured as day-time refuges.
Habits: The lesser yellow house bat emerges shortly after sunset for a short period of seldom more than an hour's intensive feeding. Insect prey is caught and eaten on the wing. When satiated, the bat will return to one of several favoured hollows in trees in the same general area where it spends the rest of the night and the following day. This characteristic of returning daily to the same area but of regularly changing the location of the day-time refuge, is probably a strategy developed to avoid predators. Banded individuals have been observed to feed in the same area nightly throughout the year, and they travel distances of up to four kilometres to their feeding sites. They appear to congregate to feed along watercourses.

Lesser yellow house bat

Diet: Beetles are taken as well as medium-sized soft-bodied insects.
Breeding: Mating takes place during early winter but normal embryonic development is delayed during the winter months and is only resumed during spring. The young are born towards the end of November or in the first half of December. Twins are common.

Schlieffen's bat

Schlieffen's bat

Nycticeius schlieffenii

Schlieffen-vlermuis

Distribution: This is the smallest of all our endemic bat species and is a common sight throughout the Park at dusk near permanent water. Schlieffen's bat is widely distributed in sub-Saharan Africa, but in the Republic it occurs only in the eastern Transvaal Lowveld and in the extreme north of Natal, where it is particularly abundant.
Habitat and habits: A savanna woodland inhabitant, Schlieffen's bat is extremely agile in flight and prefers to hunt insect prey (such as mayflies, mosquitoes, etc.) over water surfaces and in riparian forests. Like most vesper bats, it is very active during the first hour after sunset, and then virtually inactive for the remainder of the night. Schlieffen's bat roosts in fair numbers in rock crevices, hollow tree-trunks, and occasionally in the lofts of disused buildings. It has also been taken from under the bark of dead knob-thorn trees.
Diet: Small soft-bodied insects.
Breeding: Schlieffen's bats are atypical of insectivorous bats in that they mate during the winter between June and August. Ovulation and fertilisation occur in late August, suggesting that there may be a period of sperm storage in the female reproductive tracts. Between one and five ova are fertilised in each female, but owing to space restrictions in the uteri no more than three foetuses develop to full term, the remainder being re-absorbed. Between one and three young are born during late November.

Damara woolly bat

Damara woolly bat *Kerivoula argentata*

Damara-wolhaarvlermuis

Distribution: To date, only a single specimen of this rare bat has been collected in the Kruger National Park – in the Pafuri riverine forest at the confluence of the Luvuvhu and Limpopo rivers.
Habitat and habits: In South Africa this species has also been recorded from northern Zululand, suggesting it to be more widespread in the lowveld than records presently indicate. From available information it appears to be narrowly restricted to savanna woodland regions with permanent surface water and riparian forests. The Damara woolly bat is known to rest during daylight hours in weaver-bird nests, but it has also been found in the eaves of huts and amongst dense leaves in trees.
Diet: Insectivorous.
Breeding: Nothing is known of the general breeding biology of this species.

Lesser woolly bat *Kerivoula lanosa*

Klein wolhaarvlermuis

Distribution: This species is known from scattered localities over a large part of Africa. During April 1984 a subadult male of this species was trapped in the Pafuri area – the only record to date from the Park.
Habitat and habits: The one Kruger Park specimen record of this species was taken at night in a dry stream-bed in tall mopane woodland. Very little is known about the life-history of this rare and secretive bat, but it appears to occur in association with riverine forests in dry country, or in well-watered areas. It has been observed to spend the daylight hours in disused weaver or sunbird nests, in similar fashion to the Damara woolly bat.
Diet: Insectivorous.
Breeding: No information is available.

ORDER
CHIROPTERA

SUBORDER
MICROCHIROPTERA

Family
Molossidae

Free-tailed bats

Madagascar large free-tailed bat *Tadarida fulminans*

Madagaskarse grootlosstertvlermuis

Distribution: The Madagascar large free-tailed bat was originally recorded from Madagascar but is now known to be widespread, although localised, in eastern Africa. Recently the first record of this species for both South Africa and the Kruger National Park was reported from the Pafuri area where three individuals were netted. Since then the species has been sporadically encountered in the extreme northern parts of the Park.

Habitat and habits: The Madagascar large free-tailed bat is a woodland savanna species. However, small colonies take refuge by day in rock crevices, and this renders them more dependent on rocky terrain than on specific plant associations. Like most free-tailed bats, this species requires a free-fall of at least a metre before it can become airborne upon leaving the roost. It is a fast flier, and hunts for its prey above tree-top level.

Diet: Insectivorous.

Breeding: A female collected during October carried a single foetus.

Lesser woolly bat

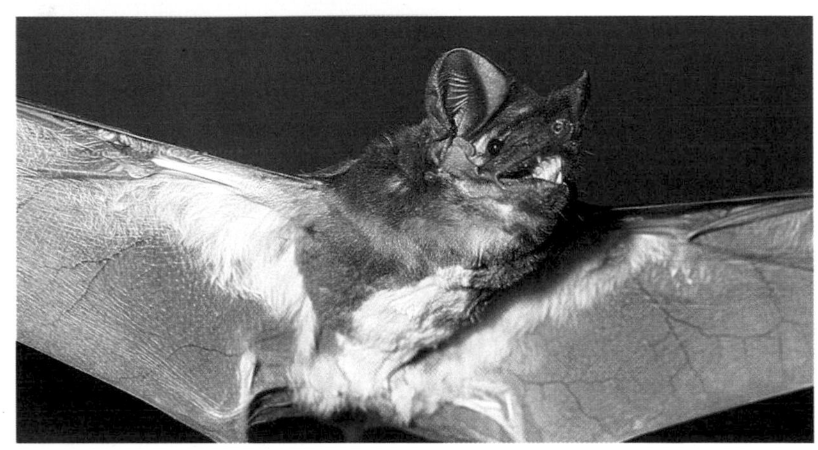

Madagascar large free-tailed bat

Egyptian free-tailed bat   Ansorge's free-tailed bat

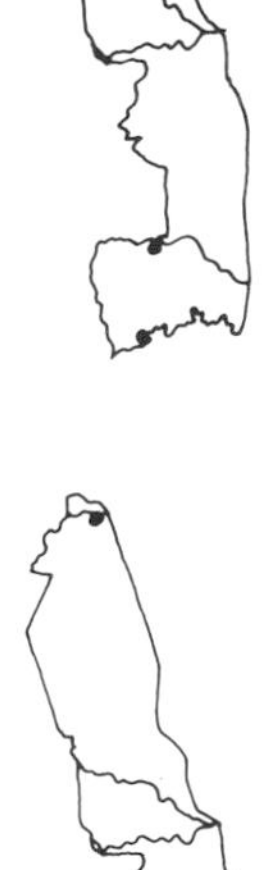

Egyptian free-tailed bat *Tadarida aegyptiaca*

Egiptiese losstertvlermuis

Distribution: A few specimens of this locally relatively rare species of free-tailed bat were collected at Skukuza many years ago by the late Warden, Col. J. Stevenson-Hamilton, and since then it has been recorded at a few other localities in the southern half of the Park.
Habitat and habits: Apparently it has a wide habitat tolerance, but is generally associated with more open country. It rests during the day under the roofs of houses, in caves, rock crevices and possibly in hollow trees.
Diet: It is an insectivorous bat, relying entirely on insects caught on the wing as a source of food.
Breeding: Pregnant females have been collected during the period September to December.

Ansorge's free-tailed bat *Tadarida ansorgei*

Ansorge-losstertvlermuis

Distribution: Although recorded only from the Pafuri and the Nwanetsi areas of the Kruger National Park, elsewhere Ansorge's free-tailed bat occurs widely through equatorial Africa, although it is nowhere common. In South Africa it is known only from the two Kruger Park localities and from the Mkuzi Game Reserve in Natal.
Habitat and habits: This species is an inhabitant of dry woodland savanna. Small colonies occupy rock crevices opening on a "cliff"-face of at least a metre in height, allowing individuals the necessary space for free-fall in order to become airborne. The species may also colonise roofs of buildings or expansion joints in bridges.
Diet: Insectivorous.
Breeding: No information is available.

Little free-tailed bat *Tadarida pumila*

Klein losstertvlermuis

Distribution: The little free-tailed bat is a common species, congregating in immense numbers in suitable roosts throughout the Park.
Habitat: It is widely distributed throughout Africa, and generally associated with savanna woodlands although it is also to be found in forests and

more arid open country. A rocky environment offering an abundance of crevices in which colonies can take refuge in large numbers appears to be a habitat prerequisite in the natural situation. Civilisation, however, offers a wide range of artificial alternatives for roosting and it seems likely that this species has expanded dramatically both in range and numbers as a consequence of human settlement.

Habits: The little free-tailed bat is a communal species inhabiting the roofs of staff dwellings and other buildings in the Park and presumably also natural roosts. Colonies occupy the same roost indefinitely and do not migrate seasonally or locally. The accumulating guano in such situations is malodorous and in buildings can eventually constitute a menace to ceilings. Individuals emerge at dusk to forage for food (flying insects caught on the wing), and are very swift in flight although they lack the agility of vesper bats and horseshoe bats. It is a favourite prey of the bat-hawk and African goshawk.

Diet: Insectivorous. Small flying insects such as mosquitoes are captured and consumed in flight.

Breeding: This species is a prolific breeder, although breeding activities are restricted to the summer months from August to April. Females give birth to only one young at a time, but are capable of three breeding cycles per season.

Midas free-tailed bat *Tadarida midas*

Midas-losstertvlermuis

Distribution: The Midas free-tailed bat is known from a single specimen collected at the Skukuza By-products Depot during February 1971, two specimens taken during January 1979 at Phalaborwa and another captured in mist-nets at Maritube near Punda Maria during September 1979. More recently a large colony was found at Gwalala in the Pafuri region. The Skukuza specimen represented the first record of the Midas free-tailed bat within the borders of the Transvaal. Subsequently, a further specimen was collected at Scrutton on the Limpopo River about 30 kilometres west of the Park border.

Little free-tailed bat

Midas free-tailed bat

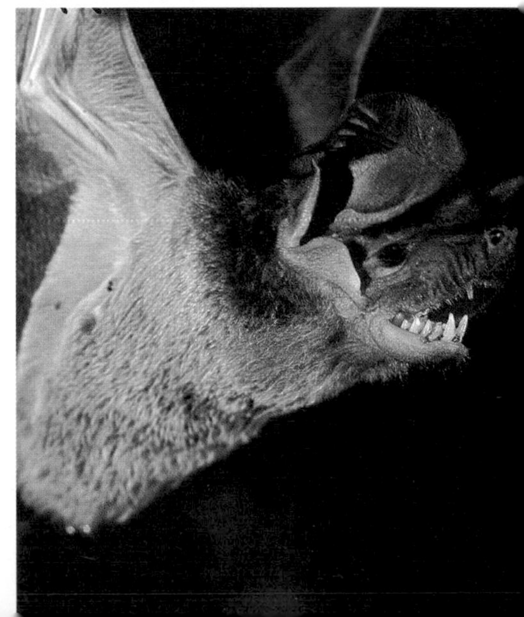

Habitat: This species favours open woodland savanna, mostly occurring in close association with permanent water sources.
Habits: The Midas free-tailed bat is communal, occurring in colonies ranging in size from a few to more than a hundred individuals. Roost-sites are occupied permanently and no local or seasonal migrations have so far been recorded. It prefers narrow crevices in which individuals pack closely together. It is very noisy throughout the day, uttering shrill piercing sounds, and emerges at dusk in small droves via regular exit-holes. Upon emergence an individual will circle the roosting area a number of times, whereupon it departs, flying high, fast and straight up to 10 kilometres or more from the roosting-site.
Diet: Insectivorous. Its prey is taken and consumed on the wing.
Breeding: The single offspring is born in summer.

Angolan free-tailed bat

Tadarida condylura

Angola-losstertvlermuis

Distribution: The Angolan free-tailed bat is a relatively common species and is widely distributed throughout the Park.
Habitat: It has a wide habitat tolerance, and has been taken in savannas as well as on the fringes of tropical forest.
Habits: Colonies ranging in size from a few to several hundred individuals rest during the day in the roofs of houses, but in contrast to other free-tailed bat species in the Park they also inhabit caves, whence they venture forth at dusk to feed exclusively on flying insects. They may also be found in crevices in rocks or in confined spaces in trees.
Diet: Insectivorous. Prey is captured and consumed in flight.
Breeding: Young have been recorded during the summer months. One offspring is born to each female. The young are naked and whitish at birth.

Angolan free-tailed bat

Thick-tailed bushbaby

ORDER PRIMATES

SUBORDER STREPSIRHINI

Family Lorisidae

Bushbabies

Thick-tailed bushbaby *Otolemur crassicaudatus*

Bosnagaap

Distribution: The thick-tailed bushbaby is sparsely distributed in forested areas throughout the Park where its weird call may often be heard at night.
Habits: It is nocturnal and arboreal, but although it has prodigious leaping powers, it appears sluggish and slow-moving on the ground. Like the lesser bushbaby it urinates on its feet and hands before leaping, an act that may also have territorial implications through scent-marking. They usually occur solitarily, in pairs or in small family groups. The adults have territories which are regularly marked and patrolled. They rest in thick foliage high up in trees during the day. Although normally silent, the thick-tailed bushbaby gives vent to raucous screams at night, not unlike the sound of a child crying.
Diet: The thick-tailed bushbaby is omnivorous, taking berries, fruits, insects, leafy shoots, gum, small animals, birds and birds' eggs. It is known to kill poultry and to take birds as large as guinea-fowl, usually eating only the head and neck. It sometimes raids the mlala-beer "factories" of local Black communities.
Breeding: The thick-tailed bushbaby has a distinct and restricted breeding season in southern Africa. Mating occurs during the months of June and July. The gestation period is about 130 days and most births occur within a period of three weeks from the beginning of November. Normally there are two young in each litter but occasionally there may be one or three. The young are born and raised in a freshly lined nest which normally serves as one of several day-time resting-places scattered throughout the bushbaby's territory.

Lesser bushbaby

Lesser bushbaby

Nagapie

Galago moholi

Distribution: The lesser bushbaby is not a very common species in the Park, but it is fairly widely distributed in woodland and woodland savanna, particularly along the western half of the area as well as in umbrella-thorn and Delagoa-thorn communities. It has not been recorded from mountainous areas. The related form *Galagoides zanzibaricus* has been recorded in the coastal areas of Mozambique to the east of the Park, but as yet no evidence of its presence has been found here.
Habitat: It is a savanna species, particularly associated with acacia savanna although some have also been taken in mopane savanna in the northern parts of the Park. It is not often encountered in tropical forest, except perhaps on the fringes.
Habits: Lesser bushbabies are considerably smaller than thick-tailed bushbabies and are also much more agile. The second toe on the hindfoot is different from the others and is adapted for grooming. These attractive little animals are nocturnal and occur sometimes singly, mostly in pairs and also in small family groups. They lie up during the day in holes in trees lined with grass, leaves and other vegetable matter, or in nests of leaves and debris. They emerge at dusk and move out to their feeding-grounds. They have regular routes along the trees, and a fairly large gap between trees is no deterrent to them as they have prodigious leaping powers (a vertical leap of even seven metres is not beyond their capacity). Their large, round eyes often reflect the beam of car headlights and shine with a reddish glow. Large owls are their main predators and their life-span is approximately 10 years.
Diet: Their diet is varied and, although consisting mainly of insects (moths, beetles, caterpillars, flying termites, etc.), also includes wild fruits, berries, tree resins and flowers. Small vertebrates are possibly taken on occasion.
Breeding: Up to three young, although usually two, are born after a gestation period of 121 to 124 days. The lesser bushbaby is a seasonal breeder, producing offspring during summer in southern Africa. There are two birth seasons in each summer, the first during October and the second during January and February.

ORDER
PRIMATES

SUBORDER
HAPLORHINI

Family
Cercopithecidae

Baboons and monkeys

Chacma baboon *Papio ursinus*

Kaapse bobbejaan

Distribution: The chacma baboon is a common species throughout the Kruger National Park and may be found in troops varying in number from a few individuals to as many as a hundred or more. Baboons are inclined to become superabundant in areas with a low density of natural predators such as the Luvuvhu and Limpopo floodplains.

The animals from most of the area making up the Kruger National Park are dark in colour and appear best placed with the subspecies *P. u. orientalis*. Specimens from the Luvuvhu and Limpopo floodplains at Pafuri, however, are much yellower overall and are better placed with the subspecies *P. u. griseipes*, which is found in the adjoining parts of Mozambique from the southern part of the Inhambane district north to the Tete district, and in South Africa in the area north of the Soutpansberg.

Habitat: A savanna and montane species, marginal on open grassland.

Habits: Baboon troops normally have well-chosen sleeping-sites, either in tall trees or on cliff-faces, from which they descend in the early morning to forage. Like vervet monkeys, the distance they travel during the day in search of food depends on its availability, but in general they do not travel more than a kilometre or two away from their sleeping-sites. They may have several such sleeping-sites within their home range and use them in rotation. Baboons are mainly ground-dwellers and are therefore vulnerable to predation. They are particularly alert and have very good eyesight and hearing. When danger threatens, the vulnerable members of the troop cluster in the centre of the group, around the most dominant and protective males, while other males surround the group, moving ahead, behind and along the flanks.

Chacma baboon and baby of the subspecies *orientalis*.

Male chacma baboon of the northern subspecies *griseipes.*

These are the males which normally give the alarm bark if danger is spotted. Baboons will often associate with other animals, such as antelope and banded mongooses, whose alertness supplements their own. In addition to the alarm bark, baboons can grunt, growl, shriek, chatter and roar. Adults may attain a mass of 30 kilograms and their life-span is about 18 years.
Diet: They are omnivorous, although largely vegetarian, feeding on wild fruits, berries, leaves, grasses, roots, bulbs, tubers and even flowers as well as on a variety of animal food such as insects, scorpions, centipedes, lizards, birds' eggs, and the fledgelings of queleas and other birds. Many instances of baboons killing and feeding on new-born lambs of antelope such as nyala, bushbuck and impala as well as hares have been documented in the Park. A few cases of cannibalism have also been recorded, as well as an instance where a new-born leopard cub was caught by a large male baboon. In areas adjoining agricultural development they can become very destructive crop raiders and they also commonly develop begging traits when they are fed by misguided tourists in national parks and nature reserves.
Breeding: Females give birth to single young after a gestation period of between six and seven months, and do not mate for the subsequent eighteen months. Breeding takes place throughout the year although most births in the Park are recorded during the summer. Cases of twins have been recorded. The circumanal area of the female swells conspicuously when she is in season. The new-born young is carried about clinging to the fur of its mother's belly and older infants often ride "jockey"-fashion on the mother's back.

Vervet monkey *Cercopithecus aethiops*
Blouaap

Distribution: The vervet monkey is commonly distributed throughout the Park with a decided preference for riparian growth and woodland or forested areas near water. A local colour variety with a characteristic rufous-coloured mane and tail is found along the Crocodile River in the Malelane area.

Habitat: It occurs primarily in savanna vegetation and the transition zone between forest and savanna, but also marginally on grassland.
Habits: The vervet monkey is a very successful primate which is able to exploit a variety of habitat types from montane or riverine forest to drier savannas and woodlands. It owes its success to the fact that it is not strictly arboreal but readily takes to the ground in order to search for food or water. As a result vervet monkeys often become cunning garden raiders and are consequently persecuted by farmers. Apart from man, their predators include leopards, pythons and the larger eagles. They are generally found in troops numbering up to 20 individuals, although larger troops are also found. These troops have a well-defined home range over which they wander in search of food. Vervet monkeys can swim well and can even dive when the occasion demands. Their life-span is approximately 12 years. Adult males can attain a mass of over five kilograms; females are lighter at around four kilograms. Cases of albinism have been recorded and this genetic trait appears to be more common in some areas (*e.g.* Malelane) than in others.
Diet: Their diet is catholic although, like samango monkeys, they are basically vegetarian; they eat wild fruits, berries, leaves, young shoots, flowers, roots, and bulbs, as well as insects, birds, eggs, scorpions and, in fact, virtually anything edible. As is the case with baboons, they become inveterate beggars in conservation areas when encouraged by unthinking tourists.
Breeding: Although the young are apparently born throughout the year in other areas, in the Kruger National Park there is a definite peak in December and January. A single young is produced after a gestation period of seven months; twins are occasionally seen.

Vervet monkey

Samango monkey

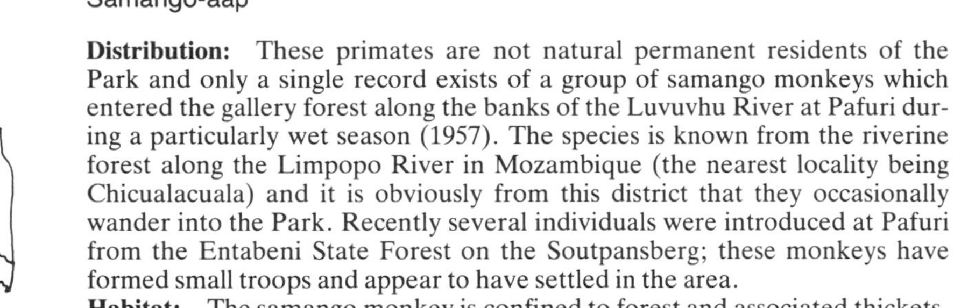

Samango monkey

Cercopithecus mitis

Samango-aap

Distribution: These primates are not natural permanent residents of the Park and only a single record exists of a group of samango monkeys which entered the gallery forest along the banks of the Luvuvhu River at Pafuri during a particularly wet season (1957). The species is known from the riverine forest along the Limpopo River in Mozambique (the nearest locality being Chicualacuala) and it is obviously from this district that they occasionally wander into the Park. Recently several individuals were introduced at Pafuri from the Entabeni State Forest on the Soutpansberg; these monkeys have formed small troops and appear to have settled in the area.

Habitat: The samango monkey is confined to forest and associated thickets. In the Transvaal it is usually associated with moist montane forests but in Mozambique it also occurs in dry forest near water, *e.g.* in Maputo Game Reserve, and in the Gorongoza and Zinave national parks.

Habits: Samango monkeys, in contrast to their cousins the vervet monkeys, spend most of their time in trees and little time foraging on the ground. They are apparently dependent on shade as a habitat requirement and are not as inclined as vervets to raid vegetable gardens and crop-lands. Both crowned eagles and leopards prey on this species.

Diet: They are largely vegetarian, feeding on fruits, berries, flowers, leaves and other vegetable matter, but also eating insects and raiding birds' nests for eggs and fledgelings. Bushbuck and blue duiker are attracted to a feeding troop of samango monkeys in the hope of picking up discarded fruits and other titbits. Bushbuck are in fact known to eat the droppings of samango monkeys, perhaps because they are rich in undigested seeds.

Breeding: A single young is born towards the end of the year, from about September to December.

ORDER
CARNIVORA

Family
Canidae

Wild dog and jackals

Bat-eared fox

Otocyon megalotis

Bakoorjakkals

Distribution: The first record of occurrence of this semi-diurnal carnivore within the borders of the Kruger National Park was made on 4 March 1967 when a family group of six were seen during the night on the road about 14 kilometres south of Shingwedzi. This penetration into the Kruger National Park coincided approximately with the appearance of the same species in the Buffalo Bend and Gonarezhou areas of south-eastern Zimbabwe (July 1966) where bat-eared foxes were also previously unknown. One possibility is that the invasion of both these areas occurred from the arid west (where it is a common species) eastwards along the sandveld corridor of the Limpopo Valley; but bat-eared foxes also occur in south-west Mozambique in an area which includes the western portion of the Limpopo Valley and the Banhine National Park further to the north and east. It is therefore equally possible that the latter area could be the reservoir from which a westward penetration of the Kruger National Park and Gonarezhou area of Zimbabwe was effected. Be that as it may, these animals have now become quite firmly established on the eastern grassland plains and mopane scrub savanna north of the Letaba River. The southern limit of their range in the Park appears to be in the area of the Malopenyana Windmill, and the northern limit is Pafuri on the Mozambique border.

Habitat: Bat-eared foxes are generally associated with open plains in arid areas, although in the Park they occur, as mentioned above, in savannas or grassland with some scrub cover.

Habits: Bat-eared foxes are semi-diurnal animals, particularly in undisturbed areas. They occur in pairs or family groups of up to six or seven. They live in disused aardvark burrows, or in burrows which they dig themselves and which may be up to three metres long. The large and sensitive ears are used to locate the sounds of underground insects and larvae. The latter are rapidly dug up with the forepaws, even in the hardest soil. The ears also serve the purpose of assisting in heat loss in the hot climate of their chosen habitats. They are extraordinarily nimble creatures, capable of doubling back on

Bat-eared fox

their tracks at high speed, and twisting and dodging as they run. This skill, which earned them the Afrikaans name "draaijakkals" (= turning jackal), enables them to run down and catch elusive animals, and also facilitates their escape from predators. The call is a rather shrill and repetitive "*who-who-who*". The bat-eared fox is preyed upon by the larger eagles and larger mammalian predators such as the brown hyaena. The life-span is approximately 10 years and adults attain a mass of four kilograms.
Diet: Bat-eared foxes are mainly insect-eaters (termites, locusts and beetles), but their diet is varied and includes scorpions, sun-spiders, wild fruits, reptiles, rodents and the nestlings and eggs of ground-nesting birds.
Breeding: Up to six young (usually two to five) are born during the rainy season in the sanctuary of a burrow after a gestation period lasting approximately 60 days.

Wild dog *Lycaon pictus*

Wildehond

Distribution: Wild dogs are abundant in the southern districts of the Park where they are frequently seen in the savanna and woodland regions of the Skukuza, Pretoriuskop, Stolsnek and Malelane sections. In the central district they are common from the Sabie River to Tshokwane, but are not often encountered in the open country between Tshokwane and the Olifants River. They are also firmly established in the broken country south of the Olifants River in the Kingfisherspruit Section. Wild dogs occur again north of the Olifants River, tending to be more common in the mopane woodlands in the western half of the Park and in the sandveld woodlands north and east of Punda Maria.
Habitat: Ideal wild dog habitat is characterised by an abundance of resident prey, permanent water and relatively low numbers of lions and spotted hyaenas, rather than by any particular vegetation or landscape type. Their relative scarcity in the central district (Orpen, Satara, Nwanetsi) north to the Olifants River is probably attributable to the large numbers of lions and spotted hyaenas found there.
Habits: Wild dogs are highly gregarious animals living in packs of four to 30 animals. They tend to be nomadic during the wet season but less so during the dry season when they remain close to water (where game animals concentrate) and to their dens (where the pups are born in winter).

Hunting is a co-operative effort in which all members of the pack other than small pups participate. The prey is not stalked, but is chased and run down, the dogs taking turns to engage in active pursuit of the victim while the others follow. The prey is savaged on the flanks and rump while still running, and eventually pulled down and killed. There is no specific killing bite, the animal being torn apart while still alive. However, the process is quick and there is little suffering involved for the victim, which by this time is in a state of severe shock.

The dogs bolt chunks of meat, and when they have pups to feed return to the den where some of the meat is regurgitated. All members of the pack assist in feeding the pups. Wild dogs usually hunt during the late afternoon and early evening and sometimes also at night.

Wild dogs are silent while pursuing their prey and only utter excited high-pitched chattering cries when pulling down an animal. They also give a mournful hooting call, usually at night, which is suspected to act as a rallying or communicating call. When disturbed, they utter a hoarse growling bark. They usually communicate by sight and smell. When searching for prey they often jump up or rear up on their hindlegs to see over the grass.

During the hottest period of the day wild dogs usually rest in shady spots, the entire pack often huddling together. They drink regularly, usually after the morning hunt and before the evening hunt, but otherwise avoid water and are reluctant to enter rivers where they can easily fall prey to crocodiles. Their reluctance to venture into water often helps prey animals to escape their relentless pursuers.

Wild dogs have a life-span of between 10 and 12 years. Adults attain a mass of between 20 and 30 kilograms. They are susceptible to distemper and mange.

Diet: Wild dogs are hunters of small- to medium-sized antelopes in the main, and the major proportion of their diet is provided by impala. They do not normally scavenge. They are also capable of killing larger animals such as zebra, kudu, waterbuck and wildebeest.

Breeding: In the Kruger National Park wild dogs are seasonal breeders with the pups being born during the dry season (May to July). Usually only one bitch in a pack is mated, and all the adult dogs mate with her. The litter of between two and eight pups is born after a gestation period of around 70 days, usually in an underground den or cave. Such dens or caves may be re-used in successive years for breeding purposes. The pups are blind and almost naked at birth. They suckle for at least two months, and are then weaned to regurgitated meat. The pups stay near the den for about nine months, after which they start accompanying the adults.

Wild dog

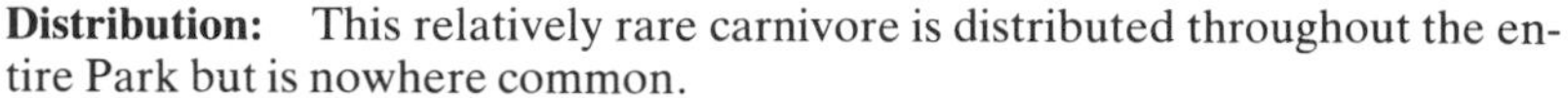

Side-striped jackal *Canis adustus*

Witkwasjakkals

Distribution: This relatively rare carnivore is distributed throughout the entire Park but is nowhere common.
Habitat: The side-striped jackal is a typical savanna inhabitant tending to be more closely associated with well-watered conditions than the black-backed jackal. It appears to be absent from the montane and forested areas of the Park and is more commonly associated with the grassland flats of the far northern regions as well as the *Combretum* (bushwillow) woodlands of the south and the tall grass areas of the Pretoriuskop Section.
Habits: These jackals, which are of a more drab colour than the black-backed jackal, derive their English name from the faint black-and-white stripe along the flank and derive their Afrikaans name from the white-tipped tail. They are larger and somewhat heavier in build than the black-backed jackal, adults attaining a mass of 10 kilograms. Side-striped jackals are not often encountered because of their nocturnal habits, but they are sometimes met with singly or in pairs just before sundown or shortly after sunrise. Later in the day they usually retire into thickets or lie up in aardvark holes whence they emerge after dark. They are generally silent animals but the call is a short yelp, "*nya*!", repeated at intervals.
Diet: Side-striped jackals are essentially scavengers but the diet is catholic, including carrion, rodents, insects such as beetles and termites, reptiles, birds and wild fruits. In agricultural areas they are known to eat mealies, groundnuts and sunflower seeds. They may become poultry thieves, but unlike black-backed jackals they are not known to kill small stock. Considering their predilection for rodent prey, they should be regarded as a useful rather than as a destructive species.
Breeding: Two to six pups (sometimes more) are born, usually during the period from September to November. The gestation period is 57 to 60 days.

Side-striped jackal

Black-backed jackal *Canis mesomelas*

Rooijakkals

Distribution: The black-backed jackal is distributed throughout the Park, but it can only be regarded as common in parts of the central district. As is the case with the wild dog, it may be vulnerable to viral epidemics such as canine distemper, and this may be the cause of the periodic sharp declines in population density. In portions of the southern and northern districts, particularly the montane or forested areas, it is decidedly rare.

Habitat: The habitat tolerance of these jackals is fairly wide and although they are commonly associated with relatively arid conditions, they show a preference for more open country; in the Park they are associated with savanna woodlands and grasslands with some scrub cover. They are less dependent on water than side-striped jackals.

Habits: They are less nocturnal in habit than their side-striped cousins, and in protected areas such as the Kruger National Park they can often be seen trotting about during day-time. They occur singly, in pairs, or occasionally in larger parties. The black-backed jackal is noisier than the side-striped jackal and its howling call "*Yaah-ha-ha-ha*" which is often combined with that of others, blends into a pleasing and characteristic nocturnal symphony. The life-span is about 13 years and adults weigh between eight and 11,5 kilograms.

Diet: The diet is mainly carrion, but also includes such prey items as rodents, other small mammals, ground-nesting birds, reptiles (mainly lizards and young tortoises), insects (such as dung-beetles, locusts and termites), sun-spiders, scorpions, wild fruits and young grass shoots. In game areas they prey on the young of antelope including wildebeest calves; they also gather in numbers at the kills of larger predators such as lions, where they snatch up morsels or feed on the carcass remains. In agricultural areas they take to small-stock and poultry raiding and develop supreme cunning in eluding the punitive measures instituted by enraged farmers. In captivity, the female is known to regurgitate meat for her young.

Breeding: From four to nine young are born in a secluded spot during spring and summer. The gestation period is between 60 and 70 days.

ORDER CARNIVORA

Family Mustelidae

Otters, badgers and weasels

Clawless otter

Aonyx capensis

Groototter

Distribution: The clawless otter is relatively common in the Kruger National Park and frequents all the perennial and some of the seasonal rivers draining the area. (*Note:* There is no positive evidence of the occurrence of the spotted-necked otter, *Lutra maculicollis*, in the Park and it should be removed from the checklist of smaller mammals for this area).

Habitat: This otter frequents perennial rivers, dams and swamps as well as permanent pools in some seasonal rivers.

Habits: The clawless otter is both diurnal and nocturnal and is found alone, in pairs, or in small family parties. The characteristic round, hand-shaped spoor is a common sight in wet sand or mud along the water's edge and the dried faeces containing the remains of crushed crabs, mussel-shells, fish-scales and bones may frequently be found on boulders in or near the water and is a certain sign of the animal's presence. The clawless otter usually lies up during the day in a sheltered area among reeds or under an overhanging bank and it also forms runs in the vegetation on the fringe of swamps. The entrance to its lair (holt) may be under water. It is an excellent swimmer and diver and usually takes to water at the least sign of danger. The call varies from a harsh chattering to a piercing whistle.

Diet: Otters are well known for the dexterity of their fingers. This is related to their feeding habits in the wild where they search under rocks and in the nooks and crannies of the river-bed for crustaceans and molluscs. The well-developed crushing molars are adapted for dealing with such hard-shelled foods. Their diet also includes fish, terrapins, leguaans, frogs, insects, aquatic birds, rodents, and even poultry. In the case of fish prey, the scales, fins and intestines are all consumed. Well-developed canines enable them to deal effectively with small mammals and birds. Their senses of smell and hearing are acute. The life-span is about 14 years and adults may attain a mass of 18 kilograms.

Breeding: Two to four pups are born in a safe retreat, usually during March and April and after a gestation period of about two months.

Clawless otter

Honey badger

Honey badger *Mellivora capensis*

Ratel

Distribution: This species is well represented in the Kruger National Park and is widely distributed throughout, occurring in practically all types of country.

Habitat: The honey badger has a wide habitat tolerance but it is not often found in forested environments.

Habits: Although both diurnal and nocturnal in habit, honey badgers are more often seen at night, either singly or in pairs. During the day they may shelter in old aardvark burrows, rock crevices or other suitable cover. Despite their superficial resemblance to true badgers they are more closely related to the weasel group of this family. They normally proceed at a characteristic jog trot. Honey badgers have a reputation for fearlessness and ferocity. With their tough and loose hide, well-developed teeth and long strong claws, they are formidable opponents when aroused, and can hold their own against several dogs. A few cases have been recorded in the Park of honey badgers being killed and eaten by wild dogs and by spotted hyaenas after prolonged fighting. More than one instance is known of a honey badger destroying the steel trap it had been caught in, and after it had ripped its way out, continuing to mangle the trap. Their bold and conspicuous black-and-white colour pattern serves to warn potential enemies that they are best left alone, and they also secrete a strong-smelling fluid from the anal glands to further deter any attacker. They growl, grunt and utter a high-pitched scream/bark when suddenly disturbed. The life-span is about 24 years and adults attain a mass of 11 kilograms.

Diet: Honey badgers range widely when foraging and they are omnivorous. Their powerful claws enable them to dig, turn over stones, tear bark away from dead trees, and even claw their way into poultry-runs. They are very fond of honey and will expend much effort to obtain this delicacy. There is some evidence that they will in fact follow a small bird, the honey-guide (*Indicator indicator*), to a bees' nest, where their climbing skills may be put to good use. They are predatory to a degree, and have been seen to hunt cane-rats and to dig up molerats. Pythons are often attacked, killed and eaten and they also kill other snakes as well as tortoises. They have been observed scraping catfish (barbel) from a pool of mud. In addition, they are known to feed on the grubs of dung-beetles which are dug up wherever possible, and they will take baboon-spiders, scorpions, various insects, eggs, birds and wild fruit. It is believed that they may attack the young of antelope if the occasion should arise.

Breeding: Mating has been observed in June and February and usually two cubs are born during spring or summer. The gestation period is about six months. The mother carries her cubs in her mouth in the same way as the lioness.

Striped polecat

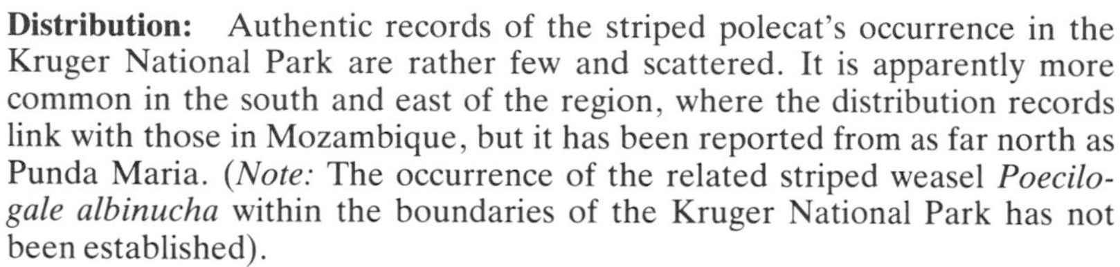

Striped polecat

Ictonyx striatus

Stinkmuishond

Distribution: Authentic records of the striped polecat's occurrence in the Kruger National Park are rather few and scattered. It is apparently more common in the south and east of the region, where the distribution records link with those in Mozambique, but it has been reported from as far north as Punda Maria. (*Note:* The occurrence of the related striped weasel *Poecilogale albinucha* within the boundaries of the Kruger National Park has not been established).

Habitat: Striped polecats appear to have a wide habitat tolerance but tend to be absent from forests and are more common in areas where there is rocky cover (*e.g.* in the Lebombos); they are, however, by no means confined to rocky habitat as they will also use holes in the ground for shelter, or the cover provided by fallen trees.

Habits: They generally occur alone or in pairs, and are strictly nocturnal and therefore seldom seen. During the day they hide away under loose boulders, in holes, in hollow trees or in thick bush. The striped polecat, like the American skunk, is a good example of an animal having conspicuous colours in order to "warn" a potential attacker that it should not be tampered with. When threatened, the polecat turns its back to the attacker, raises its tail and accurately sprays its victim with a jet of vile-smelling fluid from its anal

glands, at the same time giving voice to an unpleasant high-pitched scream. It will also sham death if necessary. The life-span of these animals is about eight years. Adult males may weigh from 800 to 1 200 grams and females from 420 to 750 grams.
Diet: They prey on invertebrates and vertebrates, including rodents, reptiles, birds, frogs, insects, scorpions, sun-spiders, centipedes and eggs. A preference is shown for insects and small mammals. They also attack poultry.
Breeding: One to three young are born after a gestation period of around 35 or 36 days, usually during the months of October and November. They make excellent pets if raised from a young age.

ORDER
CARNIVORA

Family
Viverridae

Civets, genets and mongooses

Civet

Civettictis civetta

Siwet

Distribution: The civet is relatively common throughout the Park in all suitable habitats.
Habitat: Civets have a wide habitat tolerance, but they are generally absent from forests. In the Park they show a preference for areas in the vicinity of permanent water, especially palm thickets.
Habits: Although civets are of nocturnal habit and are often encountered on the roads during night-driving, particularly during the dry season, odd individuals are not infrequently encountered abroad on overcast days or early in the morning. During the day they lie up in thick cover or holes. They have the habit of depositing their droppings in middens, the droppings being remarkably large in diameter. The secretion of their scent-glands, which looks like rancid butter, has a particularly "clinging" and penetrating odour and has long been used in the manufacture of costly perfumes. The glands are apparently used for scent-marking and assist the males in locating their mates. When threatened they erect their dorsal mane and secrete from the anal glands. They also growl deeply and give a fairly sharp cough. Civets are not normally aggressive animals but can give a good account of themselves in a fight – as was recorded once at Satara when a civet got the better of a honey badger. The life-span is about 12 years and adults attain a mass of 14 kilograms or more.

Civet

Diet: Their diet is catholic and includes rats, mice, birds, snakes, frogs, hares, insects, lizards, geckos, millipedes, sun-spiders, birds' eggs and wild fruit such as marulas. Their middens are most interesting as they are composed of a mass of millipede shells, fruit pips, bones, feathers, insect remains and other odds and ends. Civets wander widely when feeding.
Breeding: Breeding takes place during the summer months and from one to four young are born in a secluded place after a gestation period of about two months.

Small-spotted genet *Genetta genetta*

Kleinkolmuskejaatkat

Distribution: Small-spotted genets are more commonly encountered in the southern half of the Park although they are found at lower population densities throughout the rest of the sanctuary.
Habitat: In the western parts of their distributional range small-spotted genets are more commonly associated with arid conditions, but in the Park they are savanna inhabitants in areas of much higher rainfall. They have a wide habitat tolerance, occurring in riverine forests as well as dry scrub savanna and are independent of surface water.
Habits: Like the large-spotted genets they are mainly solitary animals, nocturnal, terrestrial and partly arboreal. During the day they hide in holes or other shelters and venture out only after sunset. They are wonderfully graceful in movement and readily take to trees when disturbed, where they climb to the highest branches. When cornered or at bay they will spit or growl. The life-span is about eight years and adults weigh between 1,5 and 2,0 kilograms.
Diet: The diet of this active and cunning little predator is similar to that of the large-spotted genet, and includes rats and mice, rodent-moles, snakes, lizards, geckos, frogs, insects, scorpions, sun-spiders, centipedes, birds, wild fruits and grass. It is also a stealthy raider of poultry-runs.
Breeding: The young (usually two or three) are born during the wet summer months, or just prior to the rainy season. The gestation period is about 75 days.

Small-spotted genet (note the white-tipped tail)

Large-spotted genet (note the black-tipped tail)

Large-spotted genet *Genetta tigrina*

Grootkolmuskejaatkat

Distribution: The large-spotted genet is more commonly found in the northern sections of the Park, but specimens have been recorded as far south as Malelane and Crocodile Bridge on the Crocodile River. In general, it is more common than the small-spotted genet.

Habitat: The large-spotted genet has a wide habitat tolerance but is usually absent from arid areas. Throughout its range it appears to be more generally associated with well-watered habitat in savannas.

Habits: Both species of genet are very similar in general appearance and size. Apart from certain colour differences and the larger spots, the large-spotted genet also has a black-tipped tail as opposed to the white-tipped tail of the small-spotted genet. It also lacks the crest of long hair along the backbone of the latter. These genets are usually solitary and strictly nocturnal animals which hide by day in secluded places and emerge after dark to hunt. One frequently sees them on the road at night, as they slip away into the grass. Adults may attain a mass of 2,2 kilograms.

Diet: Large-spotted genets are voracious little predators, particularly favouring rats and mice, but in other respects showing much the same prey preferences as the small-spotted genet. They are also skilled poultry thieves, and are able to slip through tiny gaps in chicken-runs. In Natal they have been reported as stealing baby crocodiles from a crocodile-farm.

Breeding: Young are born during spring and summer in hollow logs, masses of drift-wood on river-banks or other secluded places. The number of young per litter ranges from three to five and the eyes of the cubs open about ten days after birth.

Selous's mongoose

Selous's mongoose

Paracynictis selousi

Klein witstertmuishond

Distribution: During November 1986, the occurrence of this species in the Park was recorded for the first time when a specimen was killed by a vehicle on the tar road just outside Shingwedzi Rest Camp. This is only the fifth specimen of Selous's mongoose known from the Transvaal, where it appears to be rare, possibly since this is the southernmost limit of its range. Selous's mongoose is rather similar in appearance to the white-tailed mongoose, except that it is smaller and only a third of the tail towards the tip is white.
Habitat: A savanna species, absent from deserts and semi-arid regions as well as from forests, Selous's mongoose appears to favour open shrub and woodland associations on sandy soils.
Habits: Observations indicate it to be exclusively nocturnal and terrestrial. It is normally encountered singly or in pairs, and it excavates its own burrows under cover of bushes.
Diet: Although it tends to prey primarily on invertebrates, Selous's mongoose is an opportunistic feeder and will take vertebrates such as rodents, birds and their eggs, lizards and snakes when encountered. It is an avid digger in search of food items.
Breeding: The little information available suggests litters of two to four are born during the summer months.

Large grey mongoose

Large grey mongoose
Herpestes ichneumon

Grootgrysmuishond

Distribution: Apart from the white-tailed mongoose (*Ichneumia albicauda*), this is the largest of our indigenous mongoose species. These animals are decidedly rare in the Park and have so far only been recorded with certainty in the area south of the Olifants River.
Habitat: The large grey mongoose is normally associated with well-watered habitat in savannas but it is also encountered in riverine forest and bush.
Habits: While most of the "solitary" mongooses are nocturnal, this species like the slender mongoose is mainly diurnal. It is infrequently seen, however, and then usually singly or in pairs. Its abodes are secluded places such as rock crevices, hollow trees, holes, thick bush or undercut river-banks. It swims well and takes to water readily should this become necessary. A mass of three kilograms has been recorded for adults.
Diet: Its diet includes frogs, fish, crabs and vlei rats, as well as other rodents, reptiles, birds, eggs, earthworms and insects such as grasshoppers and beetles. It is also reputed to raid poultry-runs.
Breeding: The available data on breeding indicate that two to four young are born during summer.

Slender mongoose

Slender mongoose
Galerella sanguinea

Swartkwasmuishond

Distribution: This is a common species distributed throughout the entire Park in suitable surroundings.
Habitat: The slender mongoose has a wide habitat tolerance, occurring in arid as well as well-watered areas, in savannas and from sea level to elevations of over 1 500 metres.
Habits: This is a diurnal species and is normally encountered singly. It has a habit of darting across the road with the black-tipped tail arched in characteristic fashion over the back. When walking normally, however, the mongoose trails its tail with only the black tip turned up, keeping its nose to the ground and its back slightly arched. Although it is more common in well-watered areas it appears not to be greatly dependent on water as it also occurs in arid regions. It is an active and inquisitive animal and tends to investigate any-

thing new. It is a good climber and will climb trees in search of eggs or young birds, for example in quelea breeding colonies. Large birds of prey such as the martial eagle and African hawk-eagle are probably its main predators. Adult males weigh from 450 to 640 grams and adult females from 410 to 530 grams. Its life-span is about eight years.

Diet: These mongooses are adept at seeking out and killing snakes even as large and formidable as three-metre-long black mambas. Several instances of the latter being killed with surprising ease and skill by one or a pair of slender mongooses have been recorded in the Park. After making the kill the mongoose divides the snake up into shorter pieces and drags them away to its lair. It also preys on other reptiles, rats and mice, birds and their eggs, insects, scorpions, slugs and, occasionally, on wild fruits. Domestic chickens will also be attacked should the opportunity arise. Eggs are broken by thrusting them backwards through the back legs against a stone or other hard object.

Breeding: Two to three young are born in holes, crevices and other secluded places during the summer months. The gestation period is about 45 days. When they are older, young may be seen following closely behind the mother in a procession.

Meller's mongoose *Rhynchogale melleri*

Meller-muishond

Distribution: This is a relatively rare mongoose which is only known from the western half of the southern district and from the Punda Maria section in the extreme north of the Kruger National Park. A possible record of a Meller's mongoose killed by a caracal in the Letaba Section near the mouth of the Tsende has recently been reported. Outside the Park it has a wide range of distribution but is not a common species anywhere.

Habitat: In the Park it appears to be associated with montane and tall grassland areas although records are also forthcoming from the *Combretum* (bushwillow) woodland between Pretoriuskop and Skukuza as well as from just north of Skukuza. Elsewhere it appears to be a savanna inhabitant.

Habits: Meller's mongoose is strictly nocturnal and is usually met with singly or in pairs. Not a great deal is known about this species, but the wide, blunt, cheek-teeth suggest that it has a fairly omnivorous diet, rather than a purely predacious one.

Diet: Available data indicate that it feeds on termites, beetles, grasshoppers, small rodents, lizards and wild fruits.

Breeding: Two or three young are born during November or December.

Meller's mongoose

White-tailed mongoose

White-tailed mongoose

Ichneumia albicauda

Witstertmuishond

Distribution: This is not an uncommon species in the Park and it is widely distributed, especially in the area south of the Olifants River.
Habitat: The white-tailed mongoose favours well-watered savannas and grassland.
Habits: It is a nocturnal animal and is usually encountered singly or in pairs. During the day it lies up in aardvark holes, any other convenient hole, or in thick scrub. It is usually seen trotting along the road or in open spaces at night, carrying its body high off the ground, and with its head lower than the back and hindquarters. When alarmed it raises the mane of long, coarse hairs on its back. These hairs reflect light from headlamps and the distinctive white tail appears to continue as a white streak on the back. The tail is white for about four-fifths of its length. It is a terrestrial animal and is not a good climber. Although it is usually silent it can growl, bark sharply or give an explosive grunt when excited. Adults may attain a mass of 5,5 kilograms. It is said to be attracted to human habitations where it searches for dung-beetle grubs in cattle-kraals or may execute raids on poultry-runs.
Diet: In general, white-tailed mongooses have a catholic diet which includes rodents, birds, frogs, toads, crabs, reptiles, earthworms and insects such as beetles, grasshoppers and termites. Frogs and toads feature frequently in their recorded diet, confirming their preference for riverine habitats. They are avid diggers, and earthworms and insect grubs are eaten in fair quantities. Antelope dung is also taken on occasion.
Breeding: Two or three young per litter are born during the summer months, from October through to February or March. A very young cub has been found at Skukuza in November.

Water mongoose *Atilax paludinosus*

Kommetjiegatmuishond

Distribution: The water mongoose is a rare animal in the Kruger National Park and only a few authentic records exist, most of which come from the Sabie River area in the south. This is possibly misleading, however, in view of the shy nature of these large mongooses and the fact that they are amphibious and spend much of their time in the water or amongst reed-beds and thickets near the water's edge; it may be, therefore, that they are more common and widespread than our present records indicate.

Habitat: The water mongoose occurs in the vicinity of perennial rivers, streams, dams and swamps.

Habits: As its name implies, the species is associated with aquatic habitats and lives in reed-beds, swamps, or thick bush and scrub close to permanent water. They are seldom seen because of their nocturnal habits and the nature of their preferred habitat, but their presence may be betrayed by their tell-tale spoor in the mud. They are excellent swimmers and take to the water at the slightest sign of alarm, swimming with the head and back out of the water. If disturbed they are likely to emit a powerful musky smell from the anal glands. This scent is also used for marking territories. Under stress they will growl, blow loudly through the nose or emit an explosive bark. Adults may attain a mass of three kilograms. One large male measured in Natal had a mass of 5,0 kilograms.

Diet: Their food consists of aquatic animals such as crabs, fish, frogs and tadpoles, as well as mice and rats (such as the vlei rat), reptiles, birds and their eggs, insects (beetles and termites) and wild fruit. They are also known to dig up and eat crocodile eggs. The long, thin and mobile fingers of this species are adapted, like those of the otter, to feeling around in the water and mud for small animals such as crustaceans and frogs. The cheek-teeth are robust and well suited for crushing hard foods, such as freshwater mussels, crabs and beetles.

Breeding: Although there is little information available, it appears that water mongooses mate in spring and give birth during the early summer, when two to three young are born in sheltered places.

Water mongoose

Banded mongoose

Banded mongoose *Mungos mungo*

Gebande muishond

Distribution: The banded mongoose is a common terrestrial species which may be met with in suitable habitat conditions throughout the Park.
Habitat: Savannas, thickets and scrub thickets are preferred, but they also occur in dry forests and, in the Park, often give preference to rocky surroundings or to areas where there are termitaria offering suitable cover.
Habits: This gregarious mongoose species is diurnal in habit and occurs in groups of five to 50 or more members. They retreat for the night to holes in the ground or to old termitaria, rock crevices, piles of loose boulders or some other suitable refuge. These retreats are also utilised when danger threatens during the day. Being diurnal and relatively small, banded mongooses are exposed to predation, particularly by large birds of prey and for this reason thicket habitats are usually preferred to more exposed surroundings. They often have access to several termitaria or other retreats within their home range.

Banded mongooses are highly sociable animals and forage for food as a group. They chatter, whistle and croon incessantly while hunting, and their avid digging, scurrying and scraping amongst dried leaves and detritus creates the effect of bustling activity. Individuals will often stand up on their hindlegs and peer around. The adults in the colony will usually unite in attack against larger snakes as well as in defence against such enemies as eagles.

The life-span is about eight years and adults may attain a mass of 1,5 kilograms. Banded mongooses have often been seen to associate with troops of baboons in their search for food, and this form of commensalism is probably induced by the turning over of stones and dry stumps of wood by the baboons.
Diet: Their diet consists largely of insects or other invertebrates. Favoured items include scorpions, beetles and their larvae, dung-beetle grubs, sun-spiders, termites, birds' eggs, reptiles, small rodents, snails and wild fruit. They have also been seen to dig up freshwater mussels from the sand and break them in a similar manner to that used for birds' eggs, *viz.* by throwing them through their hindlegs against a rock.
Breeding: Litters numbering two to eight young are born from October to February, after a gestation period of about two months.

Dwarf mongoose *Helogale parvula*

Dwergmuishond

Distribution: The dwarf mongoose is another mongoose species commonly encountered in the Kruger Park, although they are more prominently represented in the western half of the area on the granitic soils.
Habitat: Savanna is the favoured habitat of the dwarf mongoose, as long as there is an abundance of refuges such as fallen trees, piles of rock and (especially) termite-mounds.
Habits: Dwarf mongooses are gregarious and diurnal animals which are not really dependent on the availability of surface water. They may be found in relatively arid surroundings provided there is suitable cover and sufficient food. Old termite-mounds are most often used by troops for their permanent refuges, but they also colonise rocky places or any other convenient safe retreat. A characteristic of their preferred habitat is an accumulation of dead trees, branches and logs where they can take temporary refuge from predators. Permanent retreats are recognisable by the collection of scats (droppings) outside the entrances. Where a troop has taken up permanent abode, the members will often be seen sunning themselves in the early mornings before venturing forth to feed, while keeping a sharp lookout for birds of prey. The alarm call is a sharp "*chuchwee*". A troop will circle through its territory over a period of time, using various refuges *en route*. Dwarf mongooses are inquisitive little animals and they will often sit up on their hindlegs to scan their environment. Troops may number from three to 20 or more. From their retreats they wander out by day to forage amongst fallen leaves and debris, maintaining constant vocal contact. The life-span is about six years and adults attain a mass of around 330 grams.
Diet: Insects constitute their staple food, including beetles and their larvae, termites and grasshoppers; but they will also eat virtually anything they unearth or capture, such as centipedes, scorpions, spiders, worms, small reptiles and rodents as well as wild fruits and berries. Eggs are also broken and eaten in typical mongoose fashion, *viz*. by propelling them backwards through the hindlegs against a rock to break them.
Breeding: Up to four young are born during the summer months after a gestation period of about 50 days.

ORDER
CARNIVORA

Family
Protelidae

Aardwolf

Aardwolf

Proteles cristatus

Aardwolf

Distribution: These timid and falsely maligned carnivores are rare in the Kruger National Park and sparsely distributed in the Pretoriuskop Section, the western border areas and the open grassland areas of the Lebombo Flats.

Habitat: They are generally associated with open, arid country but in the eastern parts of their range of distribution (Zimbabwe/Transvaal) they occur in more moist savannas from low to higher altitudes (from 400 metres to 1 800 metres).

Habits: The aardwolf is a shy and inoffensive animal, often erroneously accused of stock-raiding. It is mainly nocturnal, hiding by day in its den (mostly disused aardvark burrows) and venturing out at night or in the early morning and evening. It may range very far; one animal in the western Transvaal was found to travel thirty-six kilometres in twenty-four hours. When threatened, it erects its mane suddenly, which has the effect of doubling its apparent size; this produces an intimidatory effect on the attacker. It is also able to utter a loud, ferocious roar, an explosive bark or a deep growl. A third method of defence is to emit a strong-smelling odour from its anal glands. The life-span is around 13 years and adults attain a mass of 12 kilograms.

Diet: The aardwolf has poorly developed teeth and it is not surprising to find that its diet consists almost entirely of harvester- and other termites. Other insects and invertebrates such as spiders and sun-spiders as well as carrion and vegetable matter have also been recorded as food items. The teeth, apart from the canines, are too poorly developed to deal with fresh meat, and there is no evidence that it kills domestic stock. Instead of killing the aardwolf, farmers should rather regard it as a boon and offer it rigorous protection.

Breeding: The young are born in burrows, usually between September and December but sometimes as late as April, after a gestation period of approximately 60 days. There are between two and four cubs in each litter.

Aardwolf

ORDER
CARNIVORA

Family
Hyaenidae

Hyaenas

Brown hyaena

Brown hyaena

Hyaena brunnea

Strandjut

Distribution: It is not entirely certain what the status of the brown hyaena in the Kruger National Park is at present. It was well known in the early years of the Park's existence but since the end of the Second World War has been rarely reported. No firm evidence of it being permanently resident in the Park, in the form of skulls, photographs or regular reliable sightings, is available for recent years. When still regularly reported in the Park it was said to occur in the southern and central districts, but was more common north of the Letaba River along the western boundary. The two most recent reliable sightings were at the Chugamila Hills near Tshange and at Shantangalani near Klopperfontein.
Habitat: This species is widespread in the western parts of the subcontinent, occupying sparse savanna, shrublands and semi-desert areas. Where reported most commonly in the Kruger National Park in the past, it occupied open savanna and mopane woodlands in the drier regions of the Park, *viz.* those with less than 500 millimetres of annual rainfall.
Habits: The brown hyaena is normally a solitary animal, foraging alone, but several animals share a territory. Most of the animals in the territory will assist in raising cubs and will carry food back to the den for them. The boundaries of the territory are marked by the hyaenas pasting the secretions of their anal glands on grass-stems. When animals of the same sex from adjoining territories meet up they will engage in ritualised fighting. Animals of opposite sex are more tolerant of one another.

The brown hyaena is more strictly nocturnal than the spotted hyaena. During daylight hours it generally lies up in its underground den, or in the deep shade of thickets or other dense vegetation. It can live independently of permanent water, but drinks when water is available.

In keeping with its solitary and secretive life-style it is a fairly silent animal. Although it can make a wailing call it does not have the typical whooping communication call of the spotted hyaena. It also makes a rasping growl like a clock unwinding. The life-span of the brown hyaena is between 15 and 20 years and adults attain a mass of between 40 and 55 kilograms.
Diet: Recent comprehensive research on this species in the Kalahari Gemsbok National Park and elsewhere has shown that the brown hyaena, unlike its spotted cousin, is essentially a scavenger. It takes any carcass or remains of kills found in the veld as well as insects, fruits, birds and birds' eggs. It rarely makes its own kills, but when it does it usually takes animals smaller

than itself such as springbok lambs and springhares. It will often take old skin and bones if no meat is available.

Breeding: There is no strong pair-bond and females are often mated by wandering males passing through their territory. A litter of two to four cubs is born after a gestation period of 90 days. The young are born with their eyes closed and spend their first months in the den. Once they start taking solid food the other members of the group also bring food to the den area for them. They start foraging with their mother from about eight weeks of age and can fend for themselves after about 15 months. The female does not breed again until her cubs are independent.

Spotted hyaena *Crocuta crocuta*

Gevlekte hiëna

Distribution: Spotted hyaenas occur throughout the Park in all habitat types. They are abundant in the central district and particularly so in the Satara, Nwanetsi, Tshokwane, Kingfisherspruit and Skukuza areas. Further south they are also common, particularly in the Crocodile Bridge Section. In the northern regions of the Park they are less common, but nevertheless still widespread. The whooping call of the hyaena may in fact be heard at any of the rest-camps.

Habitat: The largest concentration of spotted hyaenas occurs on the relatively open savanna plains along the eastern side of the central district. These plains lie on basalt soils, are well watered, and generally support large and diverse game populations. The dense woodlands and thicket country south of the Sabie River, however, are also attractive hyaena habitats, especially in areas where there are large game populations. The northern parts of the Park, presumably because of generally more scattered prey populations, appear to be less suitable as hyaena habitat.

Habits: Spotted hyaenas live in family groups or clans of up to 15 animals which share sleeping dens. These dens may be old aardvark burrows, dongas, caves in rock outcrops and, nowadays, even man-made culverts and drainpipes. There are strong social ties among clan members and they greet one another in an elaborate ceremony which involves much mutual sniffing of the genitalia.

Spotted hyaena

The clan has a territory – an area over which its members range in their nightly foraging expeditions and which they defend against intruders. The territorial boundaries are marked by secretions from the animals' anal glands which are pasted on to grass-stems, and by communal latrines.

Hyaenas forage singly or in small groups of two to three animals. They may also move about in larger groups and all the clan members will gather at a large carcass, *e.g.* a giraffe or larger animal. They are extremely vocal animals and their most commonly heard call is a drawn-out whooping which is repeated several times. When excited and feeding at a kill or on a scavenged carcass, hyaenas utter a wide repertoire of cackling, giggling, and shrieking noises – the sounds commonly referred to in popular books as "laughing". They also utter growls and moans.

The life-span of the spotted hyaena is between 15 and 20 years and adults attain a mass of between 40 and 55 kilograms.

Adult females are larger than males and are generally socially dominant. The external genitalia of the female also closely resemble those of the male in appearance. This has resulted in the commonly held, but mistaken belief that these animals are hermaphrodites.

Diet: Spotted hyaenas are opportunistic hunters and scavengers, taking whatever food and carcasses they may come across in their nocturnal wanderings, and occasionally driving solitary lions off their kills. Hyaenas are sometimes killed by lions when contesting a kill. They are efficient hunters and will kill anything from the size of a new-born impala lamb to adult kudu and wildebeest. They eat meat, skin, bones and offal and they will even eat the faeces of other carnivores. Other items included in their catholic diet are insects, reptiles, rodents, birds, small carnivores, old or injured lions, grass, fruit and even their own dead.

Breeding: Spotted hyaenas seem not to have any distinct breeding season and cubs are born throughout the year. There are between one and three in a litter, born with their eyes open after a gestation period of about 110 days. The young are black and their adult colouring only starts to appear at about six weeks of age. They are dependent on their mother's milk for about eight months, and are weaned at about one year. They are sexually mature at about three years of age. They will follow their mother to kills and carcasses while still suckling and will join in hunting from about one year of age.

ORDER
CARNIVORA

Family
Felidae

Cats

Cheetah

Acinonyx jubatus

Jagluiperd

Distribution: Cheetahs are fairly widely distributed throughout the Park, but are common only in portions of the southern and central districts.

Habitat: They generally prefer open woodland, savanna and plains and avoid the denser thicket and riverine habitats. The *Combretum* (bushwillow) woodlands of the southern area of the Park between Skukuza and Pretoriuskop, and the acacia savanna of the Tshokwane, Satara, Kingfisherspruit, Nwanetsi, Lower Sabie and Crocodile Bridge areas are their most favoured habitats in the Park. Their preference for relatively open habitats is based on their method of hunting which is a fast and relatively short chase in which a clear view and speed are more important than stealth.

Habits: Cheetahs hunt most frequently in the early morning and late afternoon. They are normally not active at night. Adults tend to live solitary lives, but they are more sociable than leopards. The subadults stay with the

Cheetah

mother for an extended period and this accounts for the commonly sighted groups of four to six animals.

Cheetahs are the fastest quadrupeds and are reputed to reach speeds of 100 km.p.h. in short bursts, as compared with the 65 km.p.h. recorded for lions. The sleek frame, large chest, small waist, and long, relatively heavy tail are all adaptations for speed and turning at speed. The cheetah is unable to retract its claws and this may also be an adaptation to its mode of hunting.

The cheetah's hunting technique is to stalk its prey for a short distance and then to chase it at speed. Using a front foot with its exposed claws it then knocks the victim off balance, and clamps its jaws on the throat to kill by

The "king cheetah"

suffocation. The prey is usually eaten on the spot after disembowelment, though it may sometimes be dragged under the shelter of bushes.

Cheetahs are fond of climbing on to vantage-points such as ant-hills, rock outcrops or the forks of trees, from which they can survey the surrounding countryside. These vantage-points are also often marked by spray-urination.

Occasionally a genetic variant occurs in which the spots are larger and those on the back have been fused into stripes. Such an animal is a so-called "king cheetah", but it is not a separate species or subspecies.

Cheetahs have a life-span of 10 to 15 years and attain a mass of about 50 to 60 kilograms.

Diet: Cheetahs are hunters of small- to medium-sized plains game such as impala, duiker, steenbok and warthog though they also take the young of wildebeest, sassaby, sable, zebra and kudu. They are not carrion-feeders. Cheetahs often lose their prey to more dominant carnivores such as hyaenas and lions. After feeding on a carcass, beginning at the hindquarters, they will normally lie up in shade for the rest of the day.

Breeding: From two to five cubs are born in a litter, usually in the shelter of tall grass or bush; they are hidden very cunningly. The young have a conspicuous mantle of long hairs which they lose as they grow older. The mother teaches the cubs to hunt and assists them until they can fend for themselves at about 18 months. The gestation period is 90 to 95 days.

Leopard *Panthera pardus*

Luiperd

Distribution: Leopards are widespread throughout the Park but they are somewhat more common along the major rivers, especially where dense riverine vegetation is found.

Habitat: They occupy a wide range of habitats, but dense riverine bush or gallery forest such as that found along the Sabie River is ideal. Consequently there are more leopards found along rivers which provide these habitat conditions (Sabie, Nwaswitsontso, Shingwedzi and Luvuvhu) than along those with less dense fringing vegetation (Letaba and Olifants). Leopards are less commonly associated with open plains country but nonetheless can be found in savanna, woodland and thickets, being particularly fond of hills and rock outcrops with their associated dense vegetation.

Habits: Leopards are normally solitary, secretive animals. They hunt at dusk and during the night and lie up in secluded spots during the day. These may be in thickets, among tangled vegetation typical of rock outcrops and jumbled boulders, or in larger trees. In the latter case they may spend hours lying relaxed on a large branch, as high as five metres from the ground.

Its hunting technique is to stalk its prey, make a short dash to grab and then to kill it with a bite to the back of the neck. The victim is usually dragged to a tree where it is cached well out of reach of scavengers. The leopard will then feed at its leisure. It often leaves the remains to drink or rest elsewhere and returns usually in the late afternoon or at dusk of the following day (or days) to feed.

Leopard males hold and defend territories which are shared by females; there is however, no lasting pair-bond. While the female is in oestrus the male will stay with her for a few days. After mating they generally go their separate ways. When rival males trespass on a territory there may be vicious fighting and animals are sometimes killed in such encounters.

Leopards, like other cats, indulge in careful grooming and lick themselves clean of blood after killing and feeding. Their smell is less acrid than that of the other large carnivores. The harsh rasping grunt of the leopard is usually uttered in the evening and at night while the animal patrols its territory. The sound is probably intended to advertise the presence of the territory-holder to his neighbours. Like most of the cats, leopards tend to drink regularly and there are usually water-points in the territory.

The leopard's spots are usually black but a rare genetic variant with russet spots is sometimes encountered. Melanistic (all-black) leopards also occur in India and certain parts of Africa – the "black panther" of popular literature.

The leopard's life-span is about 15 years and adults attain a mass of between 40 and 80 kilograms.

Diet: The leopard is a very successful hunter of smaller game such as impala, warthog, bushbuck and also of the young of larger species like wildebeest, kudu, waterbuck and even buffalo. In addition it takes a very wide range of smaller animals such as cane-rats and other rodents, dassies, baboons, ground-nesting birds, frogs and fish; they will occasionally eat carrion. Even lesser carnivores such as cheetah are killed and eaten now and again.

Breeding: The female bears from one to three cubs after a gestation period of about 105 days. At birth the cubs are much darker and more spotted than adults. They are kept hidden in a secluded spot initially and suckle for about three months. They can tend for themselves by the age of 1,5 to 2 years, and at this age leave their mother to find their own territory. Sightings of two or three leopards together will normally be of an adult female and her offspring.

Leopard

Lion

Panthera leo

Leeu

Distribution: Lions are widely distributed throughout the Park but are more abundant south of the Olifants River. They are particularly common in the eastern half of the central and southern districts in the Satara, Tshokwane, Lower Sabie and Crocodile Bridge sections, but elsewhere in the south they are also fairly common. In the far north of the Park (north of Shingwedzi) lions are relatively less common.
Habitat: In general the distribution of lions is related to the nature of the habitat as this affects hunting success and the availability of prey. The open plains of the central district where grazing conditions are good, where permanent water is plentiful and consequently where there are large populations of plains game, provide optimum lion habitat. Lions are less abundant, however, in areas of denser woodland or more sparse game populations.
Habits: The lion is the most social of the cats, living in prides which consist of one or two males, two to six females and as many as 14 young of different ages. Prides occupy territories which they defend against neighbouring prides and against wandering lions. The territory is regularly patrolled and the presence of proprietors is advertised by roaring and scent-marking.

Young lions, on reaching the age of about three years, are forced out of the pride by the dominant males. The latter are older, stronger animals with prominent manes. The subadults may stick together and form nomadic prides, always on the move. They avoid resident territory-holders, and search for vacant areas with sufficient game for them to settle and establish their own territories.

Adult nomadic males, single or in pairs, replace territorial males when the latter become too old to defend and hold their territories and females. These nomads then take over the pride, sometimes killing all the cubs of the former owner. This stimulates the lionesses to come into oestrus so that the new males may father their own cubs.

Lions hunt co-operatively, usually at night, but also in the early morning or evening. The females do most of the killing. The prey is usually stalked from a distance and when the lion gets within range a charge is made and the prey animal is either bowled over or pounced upon. The kill is made by breaking the prey's neck or suffocating it by clamping the jaws and holding it by the nose or throat. When one member of the pride has succeeded in holding an animal the rest of the pride rushes up to help with the kill and to start feeding. At this stage the males often appropriate the kill for themselves if it is a small animal – or take the "lion's share" if it is larger.

The rare "white" lion

African lion

The kill is usually disembowelled and the entrails dragged away from the carcass. Feeding is a group activity with all members of the pride participating. There is often considerable aggression, tension, and fighting. The cubs often have to wait until the adults have finished feeding before they can get a share. In times of scarcity this may result in little food being available for cubs which then starve to death.

After feeding, lions will find some shady, sheltered spot to lie up in and rest until the next hunt, or if the kill has been a large one, until the next feeding session. Lion kills, however, attract large numbers of scavengers such as hyaenas, jackals and vultures and if the lions allow it, these will rapidly consume the remains; on occasion lions will keep scavengers away from their kill. They themselves may also appropriate the kill of hyaenas, wild dogs, and cheetahs.

Lions can swim but do not often venture into deep water. They are expert climbers of trees, however, and young lions in particular are often found high up in the forks of trees or on horizontal branches whiling away the heat of the day. They are extremely vocal and their roaring may be heard at a great distance. A full-throated roar will carry as far as eight kilometres on a still night. They also use a low cough or grunt for communicating with cubs. Lions have a life-span of 13 to 15 years. Adult males attain a mass of 150 to 225 kilograms, but females are smaller with a mass of between 110 and 150 kilograms.

A rare genetic condition which gives rise to white lions is found in the lion population of the Tshokwane area. These animals are snow-white at birth, darkening to a pale gold colour later in life. They are successful hunters and are accepted as normal members of lion society.

Diet: Lions are skilful hunters and they prey on almost all the ungulate species in the Park. In order of preference their diet consists of wildebeest, impala, zebra, waterbuck, kudu, giraffe and buffalo. They also, however, take small game, depending on how pressed they are for food. They kill and eat tortoises, porcupines, ostriches, and on occasion animals such as jackals. At times they are cannibalistic and will eat other lions. There are records of lions killing hippo in the Park and several elephant yearling calves have been recorded as being taken by them. They sometimes even attack adult black or white rhino, but with a much lower rate of success.

Breeding: Lions breed throughout the year, but cubs born during the dry season when food is more easily available have a better chance of survival. The litters consist of two to six cubs, born after a gestation period of around 110 days. The cubs are born in a sheltered spot, perhaps in a thicket, long grass or among dense vegetation on rock outcrops. The lioness suckles them there and leaves them hidden while hunting. Many are, however, taken by scavenging carnivores such as hyaena. Lionesses are usually efficient and dedicated mothers (at least while the cubs are still small) and will defend them fiercely. The cubs are weaned at six months and reach sexual maturity at about 24 months. By the time they reach three years of age they are forced out of the pride, unless conditions are such that a larger pride can be supported and the young lionesses are then absorbed as pride members. Young males are, however, driven off by the pride males.

Mating is a vocal and marathon event, and takes place many times over a period of two to three days.

Caracal

Felis caracal

Rooikat

Distribution: These graceful and rapacious carnivores have been recorded throughout the Park, but more often in woodland areas near rocky outcrops.
Habitat: In the Kruger National Park, caracals are associated with savannas or woodland areas, perhaps more often in broken country but also in grassland where there is cover provided by scrub or stands of tall grass.
Habits: They are partly nocturnal in habit but are also often encountered during the day. As a rule, however, they lie up during the day in thick bush or grass and, because of their overall reddish-tan colour, are extremely difficult to spot. They are usually solitary or in pairs. Caracals are generally silent cats, but captive specimens are known to purr very softly. Their life-span is about 12 years and adult males attain an average mass of 14 kilograms.
Diet: Caracals are more powerful and aggressive animals than servals or African wild cats and will occasionally attack prey heavier than themselves, such as impala and reedbuck. Generally, however, they only kill the smaller antelope such as duiker, klipspringer and steenbok. The main prey animals are dassies, squirrels, springhares, rats and mice, monkeys, reptiles and birds (especially guinea-fowl and francolin). The prey is stalked in typical cat-like manner with a final rush to seize or slap down the prey with a powerful sideways strike. Sometimes a caracal will catch a bird in flight by leaping up at it.

Caracal

Serval

The prey is usually toyed with before being eaten. Caracals are known killers of smaller domestic stock such as goats and sheep and are, in consequence, assiduously hunted in all areas outside national parks and nature reserves.
Breeding: Normally two young are born sometime between July and December although births have also been recorded in May, January and February. The gestation period is 2,5 months. The litter size varies from two to four.

Serval *Felis serval*

Tierboskat

Distribution: The serval is the rarest of the three smaller feline species in the Kruger National Park but has been recorded throughout the entire area. It is apparently more commonly associated with the grassland savannas and in the Park particularly, it favours the tall grassland areas of the Pretoriuskop section and the palm-studded plains of the northern Lebombo Flats.
Habitat: Apparently it has a wide habitat tolerance, although it is sparse in, or absent from arid areas and is more common in savannas where water is available.
Habits: Servals are predominantly nocturnal, and lie up during the day. They are normally seen singly or in pairs. The presence of water and cover in the form of reed-beds, tall grass or scrub bush is apparently an important habitat requirement. They look rather like miniature cheetahs with their long legs and slender bodies, but the tail is comparatively shorter. The call is a high-pitched, plaintive "*how-how-how*". The life-span is about 12 years and adults attain a mass of nine to 10 kilograms.
Diet: They prey mainly on rats and mice but also feed on other small mammals, birds (such as sleeping guinea-fowl), reptiles, insects and sun-spiders. Cane-rats and vlei rats, both of which abound in the servals' chosen habitat, are frequently eaten. They will also kill poultry and are said to catch fish. Small prey animals are usually killed with a hard downward slap of the paw and the very flexible and narrow paws are also used to hook mice and other prey out of their holes. They have prodigious leaping powers which enable them to follow and capture prey even in tall grass areas.
Breeding: From one to three kittens are born during the summer months after a gestation period of eight to 10 weeks. If domesticated at a very young age, they make very docile and confiding pets.

African wild cat

Black-footed cat

African wild cat

Felis lybica

Vaalboskat

Distribution: This is the most common of the three small cat species in the Kruger National Park and is widely distributed throughout the entire area. It is perhaps less common in the southern districts than north of the Sabie River.

Habitat: Like the serval, this species also shows a wide habitat tolerance throughout its range, occurring even in the vicinity of built-up areas as well as in very dry places. It is usually absent from montane and tropical forest areas. It appears to be very partial to mealie-fields where its principal prey items, rodents, are plentiful. In fact, man's agricultural activities have created abundant food supplies for rodents, which in turn have multiplied considerably, thus benefiting the wild cat in areas where there is extensive natural cover.

Habits: Although mainly nocturnal, hiding by day in thick cover, the wild cat may also occasionally be seen during the daylight hours. It looks very much like the domestic tabby cat, but is larger and has longer legs; in addition it may usually be distinguished from the domestic cat by the reddish fur behind the ears and over the belly and the back of the hindlegs. The tail has black bands and terminates in a black tip. The legs are also marked with transverse dark bands and the lower parts of the legs are more uniformly dark, often leading to the misidentification of this species as the black-footed cat, *Felis nigripes**. The mass of adult African wild cats varies from 2,6 to 5,0 kilograms in males.

Diet: They feed mainly on rats and mice but also eat a wide variety of other foods, including small to larger birds (such as doves and quails which are often caught in flight), reptiles (skinks, geckos, lizards and snakes), insects, the occasional scorpion, sun-spiders, small mammals such as hares, springhares and squirrels, and even wild fruit. They are also cunning poultry-raiders.

Breeding: Two to five (usually three) young are born, mainly during the summer months, although kittens have also been recorded at other times.

*There is no evidence of the occurrence of the black-footed cat on the Babalala Flats of the Kruger National Park, as was claimed by the late Chief Ranger, Col. M. Rowland-Jones. It is an animal of the arid western and southern regions of southern Africa.

The gestation period is about two months. Wild cats breed freely with domestic cats and the resulting offspring lose the red colour behind the ears. In view of this possibility of hybridisation, unspayed domestic cats have been banned from the homes of resident staff of the Kruger National Park.

ORDER PROBOSCIDEA
Family Elephantidae
Elephants

African elephant *Loxodonta africana*

Afrikaanse olifant

Distribution: The African elephant is widespread in the Kruger National Park. However, some areas have historically been associated with higher elephant densities than others. This may largely be owing to the extinction of elephants throughout the Park during the late 19th Century with the exception of a small herd in the Olifants Gorge area. From this nucleus, and from surviving populations in Mozambique and Zimbabwe the elephants recolonised the Kruger Park. The areas first colonised have most elephants today while those occupied as recently as 1952 (for example, Pretoriuskop) support the fewest. Major concentrations of elephants are found along the Letaba, Olifants, Tsende, Shingwedzi, Mphongolo and Shisha rivers, while smaller populations are associated with the Timbavati, Sabie, Mbyamiti and Crocodile river areas. There are usually between 7 000 and 8 000 elephants in the Park, but numbers fluctuate.
Habitat: The habitats occupied by elephants encompass all the vegetation types found within the boundaries of the Kruger National Park. Even the rugged mountains in the Stolsnek and Malelane sections which generally support a sour grassveld and *Combretum* savanna are utilised by bulls and a small breeding herd. Elephants require abundant grazing, browse, and permanent water, and these requirements are met throughout the Park.
Habits: Elephants are highly social, intelligent animals and they live in a well-ordered society. The basic unit is the family group or herd, made up of a cow, her older female calves, perhaps a sister or two and all the youngsters.

African elephant

The lead cow, or matriarch, is usually the oldest animal in the group. The family group varies in size from about four to 20 animals but is usually about eight to 12 in number. When family units reach about 20 in number, they usually split up into smaller groups, or younger cows with their immediate calves may split off to form a new family group.

The family relationships between groups that have split up are maintained by regular contact and meeting at water-points, favoured feeding areas and by banding together in time of danger. Youngsters from different families consort freely while families move or feed together. Several family units, all related, form a clan which occupies a particular home range.

When males reach sexual maturity at 12 to 14 years of age they leave or are evicted from the group by the older cows. They then gradually move off to areas occupied exclusively by bulls which are known as "bull areas". Here the young bulls associate with others of the same age, as well as with older, more mature bulls. The bonds between bulls, however, are not strong and their associations are usually transient. During the first ten years or so of the young bull's "bachelor" existence he may still make regular visits to his maternal clan, but these visits decline in frequency as he gets older. Bulls between the age of 25 and 35 years undergo periods of a physiological condition known as "musth", during which the animal is more aggressive, wanders over much larger areas and initiates more contacts with cows. Mating with cows is however not dependent on a bull being in musth. The external signs of musth are copious secretions from the temporal gland, and from the penis.

Within the bull area there is a clearly defined hierarchy based on physical strength and skill at combat. Bulls fight one another from an early age and thus know which animals are stronger or weaker than themselves. Fighting consists of pushing head to head with the point of contact being the base of the head or tusks. Bulls also try to press the head of an opponent down. Though most fighting is ritualised, serious fights are common and often end with the death of one of the combatants. The hierarchy is so well understood that when several bulls come together in the presence of an oestrous cow there is no competition – the bull occupying the highest rank in the hierarchy is the one to mate.

Older bulls seem less concerned with mating activities and they live quiet lives in the bull areas, associating with other old bulls and the constantly circulating young bachelors. The large tuskers of the north such as "Mafunyana", "Shingwedzi", "Shawu" and "Dzombo" fitted into this category of "retired" bulls. The home ranges occupied by such old bulls may be very large or as small as 100 square kilometres – the size seems to be determined by individual preference – whereas breeding-herd range sizes are more likely to be determined by available food resources. The Kruger Park elephant population contains a relatively high proportion of large-tusked bulls, a consequence of the protection of this population which has the genetic potential for large ivory.

Males are much larger than females, and their tusks are conspicuously heavier, longer and more curved. The forehead of the adult male is smoothly curved when seen in profile, while that of the female is more sharply angled.

As the last of the elephant's six sets of molar teeth is worn down, the elephant's ability to masticate its food declines, it loses condition and eventually dies. Elephant calves are occasionally killed by lions but predation is not an important source of mortality. Elephants have few serious disease or parasite problems, though they are susceptible to anthrax. Their normal lifespan is about 55 to 60 years.

Elephants crossing the appropriately named Olifants River.

Diet: The elephant has a catholic diet and probably eats a wider range of plants than any other herbivore in the Park. It grazes, eats reeds and sedges, herbs, shrubs, trees and climbing plants, and it also digs up roots, tubers and bulbs. It eats leaves, flowers, fruit, wood and bark, and even the terminal twigs of mopane shrubs which have been toasted to crispness by fire. It will also dig up and eat soil where the mineral concentration is high. The diverse dietary range of the elephant is made possible by its extremely flexible and sensitive trunk with which it can select individual shoots or leaves or pull down an entire branch. It can push against and break or uproot large trees, strip the bark with its tusks, or even dig up underground plant parts with its tusks and feet. Because of the large amounts of plant matter in the daily diet of the elephant (as much as 250 kilograms per day) and the destructive means by which it can acquire it, the elephant can have a significant, and highly visible, impact on plant communities. Many areas of ravaged woodland, or isolated patches of uprooted and dead trees, bear testimony to this.
Breeding: Cows are sexually mature by 12 years of age and are mated by visiting bulls who remain with the herd for short periods only. After a 22-month gestation period a single calf weighing 100 to 120 kilograms is born; twins are exceptional. The calf suckles for as long as three years, by which time its tusks are about 10 centimetres long and extremely uncomfortable for the mother. The cow can conceive while still lactating and the usual calving interval is about four years in the Kruger National Park.

ORDER
PERISSODACTYLA

Family
Rhinocerotidae

Rhinoceroses

White rhinoceros

Ceratotherium simum

Witrenoster

Distribution: Once widespread throughout the lowveld of the eastern Transvaal, the southern white rhinoceros was wiped out by hunters during the late 19th Century. Its favourite areas seem to have been the high-lying, well-watered area around Pretoriuskop, and it was to this area that the first translocated animals from Umfolozi Game Reserve were brought in 1961. Over the following decade a total of 320 adult white rhino were released in the southern district of the Park and one group of about 12 along the Tsende River in the north. The species is now well established in the Kruger National Park with the most densely settled areas being between the Mbyamiti and Mlambane rivers in the Pretoriuskop, Stolsnek and Malelane sections. They have also spread northwards across the Sabie River to Tshokwane, Satara and Nwanetsi, and eastwards to Lower Sabie and Crocodile Bridge. The northern group (which initially included only two adult females) has also done well and is scattered between the Tsende and Shingwedzi rivers.

Habitat: The ideal white rhino habitats in the Kruger National Park are well-watered undulating open woodland with abundant grass, short-grass plains, or alkaline flats with short grass. The rich open acacia savanna of the eastern flats along the Lebombo Mountains between Lower Sabie and Crocodile Bridge is also much favoured. The white rhino occupies patches of short grass in predominantly long grass areas, and will keep the grassland in a suitable condition for it to be utilised.

Habits: White rhino are somewhat more social than black rhino and groups of five to seven subadults may sometimes be encountered. On occasion such groups of subadults may associate with an adult cow and her calf, or with a territorial bull. These groups may also come together at water-holes or wal-

White rhinoceros

lows and a record-sized group of 11 white rhino was counted in a wallow at Mpondo Dam in 1981.

The well-organised social structure is based on a territory occupied, marked, patrolled and defended by a single territorial bull. Within this territory he may allow one or more subordinate adult bulls to live, and also several subadult bulls. However, they must show their subordinate status by adopting submissive behaviour patterns in his presence. The territorial bull marks his territory by scraping his feet along the ground on the boundaries, by spray-urinating, and also by kicking and scattering his dung at the middens. The subordinate bulls do not indulge in such behaviour and, like the cows, deposit their dung neatly at the middens.

Several cows and their calves may occupy a bull's territory and even that of adjacent bulls. When they try to leave the territory, however, the resident bull will try to head them back and prevent their leaving.

Fighting among bulls is accompanied by much snorting, roaring and screaming. Though fighting usually consists of sparring with the horns and pushing on the side of the head it does sometimes lead to serious injuries and death. This is not the purpose of the fighting, however, and built-in behavioural signals such as ear posture have evolved by which a weaker animal may signal his capitulation and be allowed to flee from a stronger animal without being seriously injured. Serious injury or incapacitation could well make an animal vulnerable to lions and the consequent loss of life would not be in the best interests of such a relatively slow-breeding species.

Like the black rhino, the white rhino has peak feeding periods during the early morning and late afternoon and a rest period during the heat of the day. A resting rhino usually lies down on its brisket in some shady spot, often on a watershed where there is a cooling breeze, or in a wallow. Though it may doze for long periods with its eyes closed, the ears are moving all the time to pick up sounds of any advancing danger or intruder. The white rhino has good hearing and a good sense of smell but its eyesight is poor. Like the black rhino, therefore, it often depends on oxpeckers to give their warning calls at the approach of a predator such as man. The effective range over which it can see a moving object is nevertheless greater than the range at which it can accurately identify an immobile object.

White rhino calves are sometimes preyed upon by lions, but the adults have no natural enemies other than man. A few bulls have been killed by elephants when disputing water-holes.

Bulls are slightly heavier than cows and their anterior (front) horn is relatively short and thick; the female's is longer and more slender. Adult rhinos attain a mass of around 2 000 to 2 300 kilograms (males) or 1 400 to 1 600 kilograms (females). The normal life-span is about 30 years.

Diet: The white rhino is a grazer, occasionally also taking herbs which grow amongst the grasses. It prefers short grasses and can graze almost at ground level, its broad lips being efficient collectors and pluckers of grass. The low-slung, long head is anatomically also well adapted for this purpose.

Breeding: White rhino are relatively slow breeders. Sexual maturity is reached at about five to six years of age and cows can produce a calf about once every three years. The gestation period is about 16 months, and the new-born calf weighs between 40 and 50 kilograms. The calf precedes the mother when walking or when trotting away from a disturbance, and is sometimes gently guided by the mother pressing her horn against its flanks or buttocks. The eyesight of calves is generally more acute than that of adults. They are occasionally taken by lions when still young.

Black rhinoceros *Diceros bicornis*

Swartrenoster

Distribution: This species became extinct in the Kruger National Park by about 1946. A few individuals had survived the late-19th Century onslaught by hunters, but they did not make up a viable breeding population as they were too scattered. In 1971, however, a programme of reintroductions was agreed upon, with the initial 20 animals from Natal and 12 from the Zambezi Valley of Zimbabwe being settled in the Skukuza/Nwaswitshaka area of the southern district. Later introductions from Natal in 1977 and between 1980 and 1982 added a further 38 animals. Breeding nuclei were released in the Lubyelubye area near Lower Sabie, and in the Delagoa-thorn thicket country on the Nwaswitsontso and Sweni rivers between Tshokwane and Satara. Two black rhino moved into the Park on their own from Gonarezhou in Zimbabwe. Despite some initial wandering most of the reintroduced animals soon settled down close to the release areas. The estimated population by late 1983 was 106 animals.

Habitat: Black rhino inhabit densely wooded areas with thickets and abundant shrubs, or more open country with abundant small shrubs and herbs; they also need permanent water. The areas occupied by the survivors of the original lowveld black rhino were the dense Nwatimhiri and Gomondwane thickets south of the Sabie River. There were, however, also a few survivors in the mopane savanna along the Bububu River and in the dense Nyandu bush in the northern district. The newly introduced animals have generally settled in the more densely wooded areas of their range, except for those in the fairly open country south of the Sweni River.

Habits: The black rhino is a solitary species with adult males occupying discrete territories. These territories are overlapped by the ranges of females. There are, however, no bonds between bulls and cows. The youngsters and subadults stay with their mother until the next calf is born, or may even stay on and form a threesome for a year or two after the arrival of a new calf. Young males, when they reach sexual maturity, are not readily tolerated by adult bulls and are driven off to find their own areas. This aspect of black rhino behaviour has resulted in it being mostly the young adult bulls which lead the colonisation process and move into new areas.

Black rhino are generally silent animals but they can make a variety of calls ranging from a high-pitched whine in the case of calves calling their mothers to a full-throated bellow or roar made by fighting adults. Black rhino also snort as a warning signal, and when alarmed. During a charge they snort loudly and this adds to the intimidating nature of the performance.

The bulls defaecate at established dung-heaps or middens which are scattered throughout the territory. Characteristically the bulls drag their hindfeet through their dung, kicking and scattering it about. This serves to demarcate the territory (indicating to other rhino that the area is occupied) and ensures that the territory-owner's feet are adequately impregnated with his own scent and thus that all the regularly used paths and trails are scent-marked. The territorial bull also marks his area by urinating in short bursts on bushes along the trails.

Black rhino cows and calves will also drop their dung on the middens but they do not drag their feet through it or kick it around. Cows do not urine-mark.

The black rhino is a pugnacious and aggressive animal. It will readily attack man and other predators. Its curved, sharp-pointed horns are efficient

Black rhinoceros

weapons used to impale and throw an enemy with an upward hooking action. Its eyesight is not good, but its senses of smell and hearing are acute. The large cup-shaped ears can be moved at will to pin-point the source of any disturbing sound.

Black rhino follow a well-defined daily routine with an early morning feeding period, a long resting period during the heat of the day, a late afternoon to early evening feeding period and a rest period during much of the night. Rhino usually drink during the late afternoon or evening, and at night. During hot periods they are fond of wallowing in water and mud.

Adult black rhinoceroses attain a mass of between 800 and 1 100 kilograms, the males being slightly smaller than the females. The life-span is between 30 and 40 years.

Diet: The black rhino is essentially a browser – taking leaves, flowers, fruits and twigs of shrubs and trees, but also commonly utilising herbs. It does occasionally graze to some extent, but grass is not an important part of its diet. It drinks regularly though it can go for some days without water.

Breeding: Mating is preceded by courtship behaviour. This includes snorting, growling, and sparring with the horns between the bull and cow. It may also sometimes lead to spirited fighting but seldom results in serious injury. Once the cow accepts the advances of the bull he mounts her and they mate in a standing position, with the bull's front feet placed on the cow's back. Mating is repeated several times over a period of a day or two and may last for 20 to 40 minutes at a time.

After a gestation period of about 15 months a single young is born weighing between 30 to 40 kilograms. The calf suckles for up to two years, but starts feeding on vegetation at about three months of age. While it is small, its mother is particularly alert and aggressive and will charge intruders in defence of her calf. When moving, the cow leads and the calf follows, the reverse of the white rhinoceros situation. Calves are sometimes taken by lions, and even adults that have been incapacitated in some way may also be attacked.

ORDER
PERISSODACTYLA

Family
Equidae

Horses, zebras, asses

Burchell's zebra

Burchell's zebra

Equus burchellii

Bontsebra

Distribution: Burchell's zebra occur throughout the Kruger National Park and in level of abundance rank third after impala and buffalo among the large herbivores.

Habitat: With the exception of dense shrub and tree thickets or dense riparian vegetation, zebra occur throughout all habitats represented in the Park. They reach their highest densities on open plains where they characteristically occur in association with wildebeest. Zebra are, however, extremely adaptable animals and range freely on plains with medium to tall grass (1,0 – 1,5 metres) as well as in the more heavily wooded savannas along the western half of the Park. Neither are they deterred by broken or mountainous terrain where they are widespread.

Habits: Zebra are highly gregarious animals and under optimal conditions on open short-grass plains form aggregations numbering several hundreds, or even thousands. The basic social unit in a zebra population is the small family group consisting of three to seven members. Such a family group will comprise a single adult stallion, a few mares and their offspring. Even when zebra form large concentrations the family groups remain intact and are easily discernible. In such concentrations much of the family stallion's time and energy is spent in warding off rival stallions and in coercing mares, which tend to wander away, back into the family group. Immature stallions are driven from the family units and form stallion groups.

Though zebra are capable of adapting to a wide range of habitats, they attain their highest densities on short-grass plains. Where they move into areas of taller grass or into more heavily wooded savanna the concentrations progressively splinter up until the population eventually consists of loosely dispersed family units.

Zebra may lack the formidable armoury of the antelopes in the form of horns, but are not lacking in pluck and courage. The stallions especially are adept fighters and use their teeth and hind hoofs to good effect against both predators and other zebras. Adult animals are capable of warding off most of the larger carnivores but are primarily preyed upon by lion. Young zebra may be taken by any of the other larger predators, including wild dog, spotted hyaena, cheetah and leopard.

In many open plains habitats it is common to see associations of different animal species, in most of which zebra feature prominently. The association between zebra and wildebeest – often involving large numbers of both species – is well known. However, zebra are also frequently found in the company of impala, warthog, giraffe, waterbuck, kudu and baboons.

Adult zebra attain a mass of around 320 kilograms. Their life-span is of the order of 20 years.

Diet: Zebra are almost exclusively grazers and are capable of cropping grass shoots at ground level. During periods of drought they are also known to dig out underground tubers and rhizomes. On the eastern plains north of the Letaba River zebra also occasionally nip off the tips of mopane twigs shortly after a burn, perhaps to counter some mineral deficiency in their normal diet.

Breeding: The majority of zebra foals are born during an extended foaling season, from October to March, with a definite peak from December to February. However, out-of-season births are not uncommon. The gestation period is just over one year (*ca.* 375 days) so that the mating and foaling seasons coincide with one another. Mares foal for the first time at three years of age and no cases of twins have yet been recorded. Zebra foals follow their mothers from birth and do not go through a period of concealment.

ORDER HYRACOIDEA

Family Procaviidae

Dassies

Rock dassie

Procavia capensis

Klipdassie

Distribution: This ubiquitous and well-known member of our fauna inhabits most of the suitable montane areas and boulder-strewn koppies between the Olifants and Bububu rivers in the northern half of the Park. Its absence since earliest times from most of the area south of the Olifants River, where there is an abundance of suitable habitat in the Lebombo Mountains and elsewhere, is difficult to explain. A small relict population of this species, however, exists in the Ntlokweni/Maqili area south of Pretoriuskop, in the Stolsnek Section. This particular population has remained confined to the same area for the past 25 years and has not spread to suitable rocky habitats which are available in the vicinity.

Habitat: The rock dassie is restricted to rocky koppies, hills, ravines or extensive rocky outcrops. It is of course essential that these rocky areas provide crevices and crannies in which it can shelter.

Rock dassie

Habits: Rock dassies are diurnal and gregarious, and live in small or large colonies in their chosen habitats. Dassie colonies are usually betrayed by urine stains on the rocks and piles of droppings in selected places. The crystallised urine, "hyracium", has been sold as folk medicine in southern Africa and elsewhere. Acute hearing and keen eyesight play an important rôle in the dassie's life and all members of a colony are alerted to any possible danger by shrill whistles and barks. Its major natural enemies are leopards, caracals, pythons, black eagles and other large raptors. Having no natural defence weapons against these enemies, it relies for its survival on a rapid retreat to its warren at the least sign of danger. The temperature regulation mechanism of the dassie is rather poor and shelter is also necessary to protect it from extremes of heat and cold. Hence, on cold days they do not appear outside, but huddle up in their warrens for warmth. On very hot days they will also retreat to the shade of suitable cracks or crannies amongst the rocks. Glandular secretions keep the feet of the dassie moist, enabling it to climb almost sheer rock-faces. Its life-span is about four to five years and adults attain a mass of 3,5 to 4 kilograms.
Diet: They are vegetarians, feeding only for short periods in the evenings and mornings on leaves, fruit, grass, bark and twigs. They will wander considerable distances from their rocky strongholds to feed, particularly if there is a scarcity of food. High population densities of dassies may adversely affect the regeneration of trees and other vegetation within their feeding range.
Breeding: Mating occurs during late summer. The female gives birth to between one and six precocial young after a gestation period of just over seven months. The young are born from early to mid-summer and make interesting pets if reared from an early age. They are weaned at about five months old, although they start eating solid food soon after birth.

Yellow-spotted rock dassie *Heterohyrax brucei*

Geelkoldassie

Distribution: The yellow-spotted rock dassie is a gregarious species similar to the common rock dassie, and may be found in large numbers in the broken, forest-clad hills and sandstone outcrops north of the Punda Maria/Pafuri road and along the eastern boundary as far south as Malonga Spring.
Habitat: It is closely confined to rocky koppies, hills, ravines or extensive rocky outcrops as is the case with the rock dassie. In the Park the two species do not occur together in the same locality as far as is known, although this is often the case elsewhere where their ranges overlap.

Yellow-spotted rock dassies

Habits: The habits of this species are very similar to those of the common rock dassie, and in parts of Mozambique and Zimbabwe the two species may be found living side by side in the same habitat. Caracals, leopards, eagles and pythons also prey on this species and in the Matobo National Park in Zimbabwe it has been established that a pair of black eagles can kill an average of one dassie per day. Predation by leopards can also be high. Dassies have keen eyesight and utter a shrill alarm call if danger threatens.
Diet: Like the common rock dassies they are vegetarians, eating a variety of vegetable foods. They are partly arboreal and are excellent climbers.
Breeding: One or two young are born in late summer or autumn after a gestation period of about seven months.

ORDER
TUBULIDENTATA

Family
Orycteropodidae

Aardvark

Aardvark

Aardvark

Orycteropus afer

Erdvark

Distribution: The aardvark is the only surviving species of the order Tubulidentata. It is relatively common in the Kruger National Park as judged by the number of freshly dug warrens which may be encountered in most parts of the Park, but particularly in sandveld areas with an abundance of termitaria. In view of their timid nature and nocturnal habits, however, these strange beasts are seldom seen.
Habitat: They occur in savannas and grassland (particularly those with a sandy substrate) but are usually absent from montane areas.
Habits: Aardvarks are solitary, nocturnal animals, sheltering by day in burrows which they excavate themselves, and emerging at night to wander off in search of termites and ants, their staple food. They travel long distances at night in a zigzag manner and may return to the original warren or dig a new one for use during the next day. Some of these warrens are quite extensive, with several passages and chambers. Disused aardvark burrows are of considerable ecological significance, as they provide shelter and breeding-sites for a

number of other animals, including warthogs, hyaenas, jackals, wild dogs, aardwolves and various mongooses, snakes, bats and even birds. The sense of smell of the aardvark is acutely developed and when searching for food there is much sniffing of the ground before the animal proceeds with vigorous tunnelling. The ears are folded back while digging and dense bristles around the nostrils prevent dirt from entering the nose. They are normally silent animals but can squeal if they are disturbed. Their life-span is about 12 years and large adult specimens can attain a mass of 65 kilograms.
Diet: Apart from termites, ants and their eggs which are dug from termitaria, aardvarks are also known to eat beetle larvae, locusts and wild cucumber seeds. The food is not masticated, hence the teeth are in reality functionless. Aardvarks have muscular pyloric areas in their stomachs which function rather like a gizzard in grinding up the food and sand mixture ingested. One species of wild cucumber is often found at the entrance of aardvark holes, where the animals's dung is covered over and the seeds can germinate. The aardvark's sticky tongue can extend for thirty centimetres and is whisked back and forth amongst its insect prey.
Breeding: Aardvarks give birth to a single young (rarely twins) usually during the winter months from May to August. The gestation period is about seven months and the young begin to accompany the mother on foraging trips at the age of two weeks. After six months the young begin to dig for their own food.

ORDER ARTIODACTYLA

Family Suidae

Pigs, hogs

Warthog *Phacochoerus aethiopicus*

Vlakvark

Distribution: Warthog are distributed throughout the Park, though their densities vary according to the suitability of the habitat. They are particularly abundant in the area between Lower Sabie and Crocodile Bridge, in the neighbourhood of Orpen, Tshokwane, Nwanetsi and Phalaborwa, and between the Luvuvhu and Limpopo rivers.
Habitat: A wide range of savanna and woodland habitats are suitable for warthog. Important features in preferred warthog habitats include short grass (around 0,5 metres high) areas, interspersed with patches of poor grass cover and the prevalence of wallows and burrows, such as aardvark dens and hollowed-out termite-mounds. They avoid tall grass and thickets.
Habits: Warthog are semi-gregarious and are most commonly encountered as family groups comprising one or more mature sows with their most recent piglets, sometimes still accompanied by progeny from the previous litter. Adult boars live either alone or in small "bachelor" groups, and remain largely separate from the family groups for most of the year. Sows about to farrow usually isolate themselves and drive off their former young, which, however, tend to remain in the vicinity as subadult mixed groups.

They are also generally sedentary and live in small, overlapping home ranges. Boars are polygamous and during the short mating season consort with sows and compete for dominance and mating priority by ritualised displays which may lead to fighting. Such contests of strength involve head-to-head pushing interrupted by lightning disengagements to slash with the tusks (canine teeth). Injury to the face is minimised by the two pairs of large "warts" (outgrowths of thickened skin) located below the eyes and on the sides of the snout of boars. (Sows have only one small pair of upper warts). Fights usually end when the weaker individual turns and runs, pursued only

Warthog

briefly by the victor. Warthogs are largely diurnal and sleep the night in burrows or other holes, which all but the youngest pigs enter backwards. The burrows provide protection from predators and a sheltered microclimate which compensates for the poor insulation afforded by their sparse coat of hair and minimal subdermal fat. Feeding may continue into the first hour or so after dusk, and evidence of higher mortality among males may partly be explained by the tendency of adult boars to lie up in cover rather than in burrows during the night. Mortality tends to be highest during the first and second years of life, although sows may successfully defend their young against some predators, including cheetahs. Lions and leopards are probably the major predators of warthog, and lions occasionally dig them out of their burrows. Hyaenas appear to have considerable respect for adult warthogs, which sometimes use holes within or close to hyaena den-sites. However, since hyaenas are active mainly at night when most warthog are inside their refuges, their opportunities to prey on them are restricted accordingly. Very young piglets often fall prey to martial and other large eagles. The body mass of an adult warthog is around 80 to 85 kilograms and their life expectancy is around 15 to 18 years.

Diet: Warthog are predominantly grazers, though they also feed on fruit such as marula and wild figs when available. They have powerful snouts and, particularly during the dry season, spend a great deal of time digging for grass rhizomes, bulbs and tubers. When feeding, and especially when digging for underground morsels, warthog characteristically fall on to their knees.

Breeding: There is a well-defined rutting and farrowing season. The rut reaches its peak during April and May and is characterised by the rhythmic "chugging" sound of the courting boars. Sows give birth to their first litter of piglets at the age of two years. The gestation period is nearly six months and the young are born from late October to early December. Litters average two or three piglets, though up to eight have been recorded.

Birth takes place in a burrow, where the piglets remain for roughly the first two weeks and are suckled at intervals by the mother. Subsequently the piglets start emerging for short periods until after a further few weeks they are able to accompany their mother on her day-time forays.

Bushpig

Potamochoerus porcus

Bosvark

Distribution: Bushpig are largely confined to the extreme northern regions of the Park. The highest concentrations are found in the area along, and to the north of the Luvuvhu River and in the Limpopo riverine forest. Isolated populations also occur in suitable surroundings along the Olifants River, especially in the overgrown ravines and broken terrain of the Lebombo Mountains on the eastern boundary of the Park.
Habitat: The habitat requirements of bushpig include moist forests and woodlands with dense undergrowth and thickets, and rank, tall grass and reed-beds in the neighbourhood of marshes and vleis.
Habits: Bushpig are rarely seen during the day owing to their predominantly nocturnal habits and the densely vegetated areas they inhabit. During the day they retreat to sleeping-sites constructed of plant material. In the tall grass and thick undergrowth of the Limpopo and Luvuvhu river floodplains bushpig are quite numerous and may occasionally be seen wallowing during the day.

During their foraging for food they often move away from their favourite riverine haunts and wander into broken or montane country. Bushpig are more sociable than warthog, and groups (or "sounders") of up to 10 or more may be encountered. A dominance hierarchy, established through a series of ritualised displays, exists amongst the boars. The social status acquired through the dominance hierarchy plays an important rôle in determining priorities at a favoured food resource, and possibly also in mating sequences.

Although bushpig routinely use the same home ranges, and are in the habit of marking trees in the home range by rubbing against them and gashing the bark with their tusks, it has not yet been determined whether they defend these areas against intrusion by neighbouring sounders.

Adult bushpigs attain a mass of around 60 kilograms and have a life expectancy of 12 to 15 years.
Diet: The bulk of the bushpig's diet consists of plant material, including the roots, leaves, bark and fruits of grasses, forbs and woody plants. However,

they also readily feed on eggs, amphibians, reptiles and carrion and are even known to kill and devour small antelope. Bushpig can cause havoc in cultivated lands and have also been reported to attack and kill domestic stock.

Breeding: Farrowing takes place in specially prepared grass nests in undergrowth retreats. Litters normally consist of two to four piglets though as many as eight have been recorded. They may be born throughout the year though there is a farrowing peak from September to March. Young piglets are strikingly different in colour from the adults, the basic colour pattern being dark stripes and spots, interspersed with yellow.

ORDER ARTIODACTYLA

Family Hippopotamidae

Hippopotamus

Hippopotamus

Hippopotamus amphibius

Seekoei

Distribution: Hippopotamuses are well represented in all the major perennial rivers of the Park. They also occur in the large permanent or semipermanent pools of seasonal rivers. Hippo have expanded their distribution range through the series of large dams that have been built in the Park.

Habitat: The habitats occupied by hippo are not selected simply on the basis that suitably deep water is available – the quality of river-bank grazing is also important. The most suitable water habitats are represented by pools with slow-flowing water, deep enough for the animals to submerge themselves. For all its bulk and ungainly appearance the hippo is remarkably agile and is able to negotiate steep slopes and broken terrain along river-banks in pursuit of grazing. However, though it is capable of adapting to such conditions it normally selects gently sloping river-banks, especially where these have a good grass cover.

Habits: Hippo are gregarious or semi-gregarious animals. Their territorial social organisation results in distinguishable "schools" consisting of an adult bull and a number of cows and their offspring. Schools vary in number from a few individuals to 30 or more. On reaching maturity, young bulls are driven

Hippopotamus

from the herds and lead a solitary existence until they are able to acquire a harem of their own.

Not much is known of the hippo's methods of demarcating or maintaining his territory. Territorial conflicts amongst bulls are, however, well known. In contrast to the highly ritualised displays in other species which tend to limit actual encounters – and bodily harm – to the minimum, hippo engage in genuinely fierce fighting. Using their razor-sharp lower incisors they inflict deep gashes on their opponents during encounters which may last for several hours. Fatalities from such fights are not uncommon while few herd bulls are without scars which bear testimony to their struggle to acquire a harem.

Interspersed between the schools are the lone males which have been evicted from the herds. They find sanctuary from the harassment of the herd bull in their own pools, from where in due course they launch their counter-attacks in their endeavour to take over the harem group.

Hippos are nocturnal animals. During the day they retreat to their pools or sunbathe on the sand-banks. At dusk they leave the water at fixed exits and follow established routes to their feeding grounds. As long as favourable grazing conditions exist hippo will use the same feeding grounds for prolonged periods. Their access paths therefore become well worn and assume the characteristic configuration of a hippo path, *viz.*, an elevated midstrip paralleled by two ruts, rather like a little-used farm-track with its "middelmannetjie". This is a result of the wide spacing of the legs to accommodate the bulky body.

When leaving the water at dusk hippo defaecate in characteristic fashion. The faeces are usually sprayed over an object, such as a shrub or a rock, by a rapid flicking of the tail. This peculiar behaviour is likely to have some territory-marking significance (although the fable has it that when King Lion granted the hippo the right to live in the water – as long as he didn't eat the King's fish – the hippo in return undertook to defaecate in this manner to allow the King to examine his faeces for fish remains!).

The aggressiveness of hippo is not confined to other hippo but may also be directed towards any foreign intruders in their water sanctuary. There have been a number of incidents where hippo – especially the herd bulls – have menacingly charged boats, and even capsized them. A number of years ago there was an unfortunate incident in the Pafuri area when a hippo killed a man on dry land by charging him down and biting him in half.

By virtue of their size hippo have very few natural enemies and mature animals can only be preyed upon by lion. Young calves may, however, fall prey to hyaena and crocodile.

Adult hippopotamuses attain a mass of around 1 500 kilograms, the bulls being slightly heavier than the cows. They have a life expectancy of 40 to 50 years.

Diet: Hippo are exclusively grazers. They are partial to short grass areas where their broad, flat lips enable them to crop the grass at ground level. Where hippo regularly feed on river-banks and these areas are not overutilised, the cropping of the grass results in "lawns" developing – especially where such creeping species as *Cynodon dactylon* ("kweek") are common.

Breeding: After a gestation period of only eight months a single calf is born. Hippo calves may be born throughout the year though there is a seasonal peak during the summer months. Prior to giving birth the hippo cow leaves the herd and gives birth to her calf in suitable cover, perhaps in a dense reed-bed. The cow and calf remain in isolation for some time before rejoining the herd.

Giraffe

Giraffe

Giraffa camelopardalis

Kameelperd

Distribution: Giraffe are widely distributed throughout most of the Park, though their densities vary considerably. They attain their highest concentrations in the area between the Sabie and Olifants rivers, and are also common south of the former. North of the Olifants River they are plentiful in the area around Olifants Rest Camp but are rare further northwards. North of Punda Maria they are almost totally absent.

Habitat: Giraffe occur in most savanna habitats, especially those dominated by, or with a high proportion of acacia species, particularly knobthorn, umbrella-thorn and Delagoa-thorn.

Habits: Semi-gregarious by nature, giraffe are encountered singly (mostly old bulls) or in small groups of two to six animals. These groups may consist of males only, females and their young, or groups of mixed sexes and ages. The incidence of single males and "bachelor" groups in peripheral areas of less suitable habitat, where giraffe occur in low densities, is especially striking, as the cows and their offspring are, appropriately, proportionately more prominent in the best giraffe habitats. Loose associations of 30 to 40 giraffe are also occasionally seen, mostly apparently as a result of a restricted or favoured food resource rather than because social ties exist. Areas with high giraffe concentrations are readily recognisable by the characteristic rounded or "hour-glass" shape of their favoured tree species, which they can "prune" to a height of five metres.

Giraffe feature high as a preferred prey species of the lion – the only predators of any consequence for adult giraffe. However, giraffe can deliver devastating blows with their forelegs and several cases are on record of lions coming off second best from such encounters.

Fighting amongst giraffe bulls is not uncommon. During such a fight the two bulls stand alongside one another and, in seemingly leisurely fashion, alternately strike at each other with the head – the objective being to sway the head under the neck of the opponent and strike him on the opposite flank with the short stout horns.

Giraffe are sociable animals and are often seen in association with impala, baboons, wildebeest, zebra, kudu and other game species of open savannas. They are normally silent and though they are reported to utter low calls in certain circumstances, these are rarely heard.

The giraffe is the tallest animal in the world, males averaging 4,9 to 5,2 metres in total height, and about 3,3 metres to the shoulder. Females achieve total heights of 4,3 to 4,6 metres. Bull giraffes are also considerably heavier than the cows and attain a mass of between 970 and 1 400 kilograms in the Transvaal; cows attain a mass of 700 to 950 kilograms. Their colour tends to darken with age and they have a life-span of between 20 and 30 years.

Diet: Giraffe are almost exclusively browsers. They have also been seen to chew on old bones – possibly because of a mineral deficiency – and to take the occasional bite of grass.

Breeding: Giraffe normally give birth to one calf, but a single incidence of still-born twins is on record from a private nature reserve adjoining the Park. They give birth for the first time at the age of five to six years. The gestation period is 15 months and calves are born throughout the year, with no clear indication of calving peaks. Within a few hours of birth the calf is strong and agile enough to follow its mother.

ORDER ARTIODACTYLA

Family Bovidae

Buffalo, antelope, gazelles

Blue wildebeest *Connochaetes taurinus*

Blouwildebees

Distribution: Wildebeest are widely distributed throughout the Park though their densities vary considerably from one area to another, depending on the suitability of the habitat. Throughout most of their range north of the Olifants River they occur as scattered herds – or minor local concentrations on the eastern plains – but nowhere in any significant numbers. South of the Olifants River there are three major concentrations, *viz.*, (i) in the area to the north-east of Satara (Mavumbye/Gudzani/Bangu), (ii) between the Sweni River and Mlondozi Dam and (iii) on the open plains between Lower Sabie and Crocodile Bridge. Vestiges of a largely reduced population that once inhabited the area along the western boundary are still apparent in the Orpen Gate area, as well as around Pretoriuskop.

Habitat: Wildebeest are partial to open short-grass (*ca.* 0,1 metre high) plains or lightly wooded open savanna habitats. During periods of above-average rainfall when their favoured grasslands have become rank and tall, it has been noticed that they tend to select areas with higher tree and shrub densities but with short grass, rather than remain in the tall grass areas.

Habits: Wildebeest are highly gregarious animals and under optimal habitat conditions form concentrations numbering several hundreds and even thousands. When such conditions prevail there is normally a great deal of activity amongst the adult bulls, which establish territories and attempt to retain a group of females and young. Breeding herds, however, are not confined to a particular bull's territory and move freely from one to the next. There is also a free exchange of individuals in the breeding herds and consequently there are no stable social groupings.

Large concentrations of wildebeest frequently undertake cyclic annual migrations which coincide with the wet summer season and dry winter season. These migrations follow fixed patterns, with the same wet- and dry-season

Blue wildebeest

concentration areas being used in successive years. In the Park the major concentrations make up discrete subpopulations with minimal intermixing between adjoining concentrations. Nevertheless a significant proportion of the wildebeest population consists of scattered, sedentary herds which do not migrate. These are normally smaller herds consisting of fewer than 10, to as many as 30 or 40 individuals and are accompanied by a single adult male.

Young wildebeest males are evicted from the breeding herds at the age of one year. Once on their own, the young males form "bachelor" groups which may consist of two or three, or up to 40 individuals, or more.

Territorial males maintain their dominance over other males by means of elaborate ritualised displays, in which the head, ears, tail and general posture of the body play an important rôle. Posturing is primarily intended as a show of strength but should this not succeed in discouraging either of the two rivals, fighting will ensue. Fighting consists of a fierce pushing duel with both contenders on their knees, but does not cause bodily harm. Territorial bulls are highly vulnerable to predation and significantly more adult males are caught by lions than other age or sex groups. Subadult wildebeest are preyed upon by all the other large predators, including leopard, cheetah, spotted hyaena and wild dogs.

Cows do not leave the herds to give birth. Despite the awkward, gawky appearance of newly born calves they gain strength in a remarkably short time and within a few hours are strong and agile enough to follow their mothers. They do not conceal themselves, as some antelope do, and when older form cohesive nurseries and spend most of their time together.

Adult wildebeest attain a mass of about 250 kilograms; their life-span is around 15 to 20 years.

Diet: Blue wildebeest feed exclusively on grasses, and are not known to browse or feed on forbs. They can in fact feed on extremely short grass and where they occur in high densities under optimal conditions their grazing grounds are often virtually denuded of grass over extensive areas. They are also readily attracted to freshly burned areas with the first signs of young shoots.

Breeding: The well-defined calving season commences at the end of November and continues to the end of January. Cows give birth to a single calf and no confirmed cases of twins have been recorded. The light, fawn-coloured calves are strikingly different from the adults. Cows give birth for the first time at the age of three years.

Lichtenstein's hartebeest

Sigmoceros lichtensteinii

Lichtenstein-hartbees

Distribution: Lichtenstein's hartebeest became extinct in the Republic during the present century, the last group surviving in the Klaserie district until around 1954. With the exception of this isolated – and little-known – group the rest of the population had apparently become extinct by the early 1930s.

In 1985 the National Parks Board embarked on an ambitious project to re-introduce Lichtenstein's hartebeest to the Park. The closest population from which a number of animals could be obtained was in Malaŵi. In July 1985 six animals were successfully translocated and released in a large enclosure some 25 kilometres south of Punda Maria on the eastern basalt plains. Since its release this small group of animals has adapted well to its new environment and two calves have been born in the enclosure (as of December 1986). In November 1986 a further 15 Lichtenstein's hartebeest, also flown in from Malaŵi, were released into the enclosure to supplement the herd.

Habits: From studies undertaken in Zimbabwe and Zambia, it would appear that Lichtenstein's hartebeest closely resembles the sassaby in terms of social organisation and behavioural patterns. The species is semi-gregarious by nature and the herds seldom number more than 10, consisting of a herd bull, together with a number of adult cows, immatures and juveniles. Young males are evicted from the breeding herds by the age of one year. The evicted males may associate in small groups of two to four, but a large proportion of the evicted bulls are singletons.

Lichtenstein's hartebeest have a territorial social organisation similar to that described for the sassaby (p. 117). Each herd occupies a territory and conflict between rival males is largely confined to ritualised displays.

Both sexes have horns and are similar in appearance. The males, however, are slightly heavier than the females and attain a mass of between 160 and 200 kilograms.

Diet: Though relatively little is known of the feeding habits of Lichtenstein's hartebeest, its diet appears to consist largely, if not exclusively, of grass.

Breeding: In Zimbabwe and Mozambique there is a well-defined calving season with the peak calving period in September, much the same as for sassaby in the Kruger Park. Cows calve for the first time at two years of age and give birth to a single calf.

Lichtenstein's hartebeest

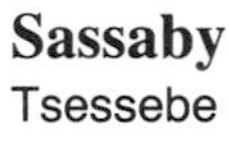

Sassaby
Damaliscus lunatus

Tsessebe

Distribution: The highest density of sassaby is found on the extensive basalt plains in the eastern half of the Park, north of the Letaba River. Scattered herds also occur in the more heavily wooded savanna on granitic soils in the adjacent western half. South of the Letaba River sassaby are only found in low numbers and as isolated, scattered herds in the west and in the Mlondozi Dam area in the east. Efforts are under way to reintroduce sassaby to the Pretoriuskop area, where they were extirpated in the earlier half of this century. Historically they also occurred on the Lebombo plains between Lower Sabie and the Crocodile River.

Habitat: Sassaby have a marked predilection for open, lightly wooded savanna plains, with medium-tall (0,5 to 1,0 metres) grasses. They avoid heavily utilised and trampled areas, or situations with dense tree or shrub stands or both. Where they occur in the western half of the Park in more heavily wooded savanna, they are associated with the more open lower-lying areas with fewer trees and shrubs.

Habits: Sassaby are semi-gregarious and associate in herds numbering from four to 10, occasionally more than 10, but only exceptionally more than 15. Each herd is accompanied by a single mature bull. A dominance hierarchy exists amongst the females and the most dominant cow leads the herd. Because of the dominance/subordinancy relationships amongst the members of a herd, cows are not accepted in other herds without unleashing a hostile reaction from the herd members of similar or higher social standing. This system ensures a high degree of stability in the breeding herds.

Sassaby bulls establish territories with definite boundaries. Demarcation of the boundaries is primarily accomplished by means of small and scattered dung-heaps which are maintained by regular patrolling. Secretions from the pre-orbital glands situated below the eyes are rubbed on to certain objects, *e.g.* twigs and branches, to serve as additional territory demarcators while secretions from the glands between the hoofs of the forefeet provide scent "markers" wherever the bulls walk. A territorial bull actively defends his territory from intrusion by any other sassaby males. In the Park the territory of a sassaby bull is large enough to incorporate the home range of a breeding herd and consequently the population is dispersed as self-contained discrete units spread throughout their favoured habitats. This is in contrast to certain high-density sassaby areas elsewhere where the territories are smaller and breeding herds of females are not confined to a single territory.

Young males are evicted from the breeding herds at the age of one year. The eviction process takes two to three weeks, during which time the bull relentlessly pursues the young male at high speed and over long distances until the youngster's family ties are eventually severed. The evicted males group together in "bachelor" herds that roam about in peripheral areas, between established territories. At the age of four to five years the young males are able to attempt to set up their own breeding herds.

Territorial bulls establish dung-heaps and frequently parade themselves on termite-mounds or other suitable vantage-points. This behaviour is intended to advertise the presence of the territory's proprietor and intimidate would-be rivals. Should these warnings be ignored and two bulls clash, fighting initially consists of ritualised displays. Standing close to one another, they throw their heads in violent up-and-down movements until they eventually fall on their knees and engage in a vicious pushing duel. Fighting is not intended to do bodily harm, but rather to establish which is the stronger contender after which the subordinate male jumps up and hastily beats a retreat.

Sassaby calves club together in nurseries shortly after they are born. They are not concealed after birth but frequently lie down close to their mothers while the latter are grazing. In their first few weeks the calves often lie together in the company of an adult cow while the herd moves away to drink.

Adult sassaby are preyed upon by lion and occasionally also by leopard. Subadults are additionally vulnerable to predation by cheetah, spotted hyaena and wild dog.

Both sexes have horns and the males are slightly larger than the females. Adults achieve a mass of about 140 kilograms and they have a life-span of 12 to 15 years.

Diet: Sassaby feed almost exclusively on grasses. They are not known to browse, and apparently only incidentally feed on forbs. Although they are attracted to short grass areas especially where there are sprouting green shoots following a burn, sassaby normally select the upper parts of grass tussocks.

Breeding: Sassaby are strictly seasonal breeders. The rutting season commences in January and lasts until March. The calving season follows from mid-September to early November. The calves are light fawn at birth. Singletons are the rule and no records of twins have yet been confirmed. Cows have their first calf at the age of three years.

Red duiker *Cephalophus natalensis*

Rooiduiker

Distribution: The only area harbouring a natural population of red duiker in the Park was excised in the 1960s as a result of unavoidable boundary realignments. To maintain the red duiker as part of the fauna of the Kruger National Park a number were translocated from the Nelshoogte, Mariepskop and Hluhluwe areas and successfully established in suitable areas around Pretoriuskop and along the Sabie River.

Habitat: Red duiker are partial to evergreen, moist forests and ravines with dense undergrowth.

Habits: They are restricted to heavily overgrown forests and are very secre-

Red duiker

Common duiker

tive by nature. Consequently little is known of their habits. They are generally encountered singly, and probably only form pair-bonds during the mating season. Communal dung-heaps are used and there are strong indications that the males, and possibly also the females, are territorial.

Both sexes have horns and look alike. Adults attain a mass of about 14 kilograms and have a life-span of some eight to 10 years.

Diet: Though they are primarily browsers, red duiker may also feed on young grass shoots.

Breeding: Too little is known of either their reproduction or associated behaviour to merit comment.

Common duiker *Sylvicapra grimmia*

Gewone duiker

Distribution: Common duiker are widespread and relatively common throughout the Park.

Habitat: Moderate to dense thickets and undergrowth are an important feature of common duiker habitats. They are commonly found in the riparian vegetation of rivers and dry watercourses but are not restricted to such areas. They avoid open plains and hilly terrain.

Habits: Little is known of the social organisation and behaviour of these shy and retiring little animals. They are most often found singly but occasionally also in pairs. The same individual will occupy a particular area for prolonged periods, probably for as long as conditions remain favourable. This habit, taken together with its possession of a pair of well-developed pre-orbital glands which are used in so many other species for scent-marking territories, would suggest that the common duiker may also be territorial.

When disturbed, common duiker only trot away from the source of danger at first, but break into a series of darting, zigzag leaps and bounds into dense undergrowth if further pursued.

Only the males have horns and the females are slightly larger than the males. They attain a mass of 18 to 20 kilograms.

Diet: Common duiker are exclusively browsers and utilise a wide variety of forbs and shrubs as also the fruits and leaves that fall from trees.
Breeding: Cases of twins have been recorded for common duiker although they usually give birth to a single lamb. Though there appear to be lambing peaks, young are born throughout the year. Lambs remain concealed for some time after birth before accompanying their mothers.

Klipspringer *Oreotragus oreotragus*

Klipspringer

Distribution: Klipspringer are widely distributed throughout the Park.
Habitats: As their name implies they are partial to rocky outcrops and boulder-strewn hills, and are in fact restricted to such habitats.
Habits: Klipspringer occur singly, in pairs or as small family groups. The males are territorial and establish their territories by scent-marking and ritualised displays. The large pre-orbital glands are very prominent and the black exudate is deposited on twigs and similar objects throughout the territories. Females also participate in the marking process and assist the male in defending the territory from intrusion by other klipspringer.

One of the most interesting aspects of its biology is its adaptation to rocky habitats. The agility and speed with which it bounds from one rock to another is astounding. This ability is made possible by the feet which have evolved in such a way as to allow klipspringer to move about on the tips of their somewhat rubbery hoofs.

The vantage-points offered by the rocky hills inhabited by klipspringer are put to good use as outlooks from which predators may be detected, or for advertising their territories, or both. Klipspringer normally rest under cover from where they can easily scan the surrounding area, or stand motionless for long periods on a high or protruding rock. If danger is sensed they emit a sharp high-pitched alarm call. When the alarm is raised other klipspringer in the area will also take up vantage-points and utter the alarm call if they feel threatened.

In the environments they inhabit, the major predators of klipspringer are leopards, pythons, martial eagles and black eagles.

Only male klipspringers have horns and the females are slightly larger than the males. Adults attain a mass of around 12 kilograms and they have a lifespan of about eight to 10 years.

Klipspringer

Oribi

Diet: The klipspringer's diet consists predominantly of browse, with only a limited amount of grass being taken. A wide variety of shrubs and trees are browsed.
Breeding: A single lamb is the norm and no cases of twins have been recorded. There is no evidence of a fixed breeding season and lambs are born throughout the year. For the first three to four months the lambs remain concealed and do not accompany their mothers. Once they are weaned the mother/young bond is broken and the young are driven from the territory.

Oribi

Ourebia ourebi

Oorbietjie

Distribution: The distribution of oribi in the Park is limited to the higher altitude landscapes in the extreme south-western areas around Pretoriuskop. From archival records it is apparent that in days gone by they were more commonly found in the area to the west of the Park, outside its boundaries, and that their occurrence in the Park is only marginal. In the first half of the 1970s a number of oribi were caught in the Amsterdam area of the eastern Transvaal Highveld and translocated to the Pretoriuskop area to augment the very low-density natural population.
Habitat: Oribi characteristically frequent open grasslands with medium to tall grasses and patches of short grass. They do not occur in heavily wooded areas and are not partial to open plains with extensive areas of short grass.
Habits: Solitary rams are frequently encountered though oribi are commonly found in pairs or small family groups of up to four to six animals. Larger temporary associations of two or more family groups are also occasionally seen.

Oribi rams demarcate and defend territories. This behaviour is especially apparent during the restricted rutting season. Demarcation is primarily achieved through the deposition of the exudate of the pre-orbital gland on to objects such as grass-stalks, twigs and so on. The communal dung-heaps, used by all the individuals of a group, have no significance in the marking of territories.

In common with most of the other small antelopes, oribi rely heavily on concealment in the avoidance of predators. When resting they retire to an area of suitable cover but also select vantage-points from where they can scan the surrounding area. If approached they remain motionless and are only flushed at close quarters. When flushed they dart off for a few hundred metres with the short dark-brown tail held erect and then take refuge in cover where they again "freeze" in an attempt to foil their pursuers.

Although oribi may be preyed upon by all the large carnivores, they mainly fall prey to cheetah, and occasionally leopard. They may also be preyed upon by pythons and martial eagles.

Only male oribi have horns and the females are slightly larger than the males. Adults attain a mass of about 14 kilograms and their life-span is between eight and 10 years.

Diet: Grasses make up the bulk of the oribi's diet while browse, if any, is taken in limited quantities. Oribi are readily attracted to the tender green growth following a veld fire.

Breeding: A single lamb is born after a gestation period of seven months. No cases of twins have been recorded. The young are born in an extended lambing season which corresponds with the summer months. Lambs remain concealed after birth and do not join up with the family group before they are approximately three months of age.

Steenbok *Raphicerus campestris*

Steenbok

Distribution: Steenbok are widely distributed throughout the Park, though they occur in higher densities in the open plains in the eastern districts.

Habitat: The presence of steenbok in a large variety of habitats ranging from open plains to open woodlands and thickets, and from undulating country to broken and hilly terrain, illustrates their ability to adapt to widely differing situations. They do, however, attain their highest densities in the open plains habitat with short to medium-tall grasses interspersed with shrubs.

Habits: Though steenbok are frequently seen in pairs they are essentially solitary animals. In fact, the only time when there is some form of a pair-bond between adults is during the brief courtship and mating period.

Both males and females are territorial and occupy their own individual territories. The territories do, however, overlap and should a female enter an adjoining male's territory, the male will approach the female in courtship fashion to determine whether she is in oestrus or not. If she is not in oestrus, each goes its own way without any attachment to the other. It is usually from these brief encounters that one may get the impression that steenbok associate in pairs.

Large active pre-orbital glands (just below the eye) are present in both sexes. Contrary to the case in many other territorial species, these glands apparently play no rôle in territorial demarcation. Steenbok do, however, possess well-developed intermandibular glands – situated between the two halves of the lower jaw – which are used for marking their territories. A steenbok may frequently be seen to lift its head and "scratch" its throat on a twig, grass stubble or on other similar objects. This apparent scratching is, in fact, a deliberate action to transfer the glandular exudate to the object and in that way mark its territory.

The territories encompass some 30 hectares and are therefore relatively large for such small antelope.

Steenbok are diurnal animals and are mostly active from early to mid-morning and again in the late afternoon. During the heat of the day they take cover in the shade of a shrub or a stand of tall grass. When approached they often rely on "freezing" to avoid attracting attention and are only flushed at close quarters and when approached directly.

On rare occasions steenbok will drink, though they are to all intents and purposes independent of surface water.

Steenbok are vulnerable to all the larger carnivores but more particularly fall prey to the middle-order carnivores including cheetah, wild dog, pythons and even martial eagles.

Only male steenbok have horns and females are slightly larger than the males. Adults attain a mass of around 11 kilograms and have a life-span of six to 10 years.

Diet: Steenbok are predominantly browsers and feed on a wide variety of forbs and shrubs with grasses normally constituting less than half of their diet. The high incidence of forbs in their diet and their preference for open plains habitats render steenbok ideally suited to moderately disturbed or overutilised rangelands.

Breeding: Gestation lasts five to six months and lambs are born throughout the year. Normally a female gives birth to one lamb only and very rarely to twins. Lambs remain concealed for the first three months, finding cover in aardvark holes or in stands of grass or shrubs, after which they follow their mothers. At the age of one year, when the young steenbok become sexually mature, the territorial instincts of the adolescents lead to conflicts with their dams and the mother/young bond is severed.

Steenbok

Sharpe's grysbok

Sharpe's grysbok *Raphicerus sharpei*

Sharpe-grysbok

Distribution: Though Sharpe's grysbok (also known as Sharpe's steenbok) are widespread throughout the Kruger National Park, their distribution pattern is patchy. Their major area of occupation stretches along the eastern half of the Park.
Habitat: Unlike steenbok, Sharpe's grysbok are rather particular in their habitat preferences. They are commonly found in broken and hilly country and in woodlands and savannas along watercourses. They have a preference for semi-arid areas and normally inhabit areas with low ground cover.
Habits: No detailed ecological study has, as yet, been undertaken on this shy and timid antelope and consequently little is known of its social organisation and other habits. Generally, it appears to be very similar to steenbok in most respects. It is commonly encountered singly and also has the habit of lying-up and "freezing" when approached; it only darts away at high speed when danger is most imminent. Unlike the steenbok, however, it is essentially nocturnal in habit. It falls prey to the same carnivores as the steenbok.

Only male Sharpe's grysbok have horns and the females are slightly larger than the males. Adults attain a body mass of about eight kilograms and have a life-span of six to 10 years.
Diet: The little that is known of the food preferences of Sharpe's grysbok suggests that it predominantly feeds on browse but that it may also graze to some extent.
Breeding: There is no evidence of a specific lambing season, and the mother/infant relationship closely resembles that of the steenbok.

Suni *Neotragus moschatus*

Soenie

Distribution: Suni are extremely rare in the Park and the only confirmed records are from the dense thicket communities of sand camwood in the extreme north-eastern areas. They are, however, reported to be more common in the ironwood woodlands in the adjoining areas of Mozambique. Attempts

to augment the existing population with transfers of suni from Natal have met with limited success so far, mainly because of problems in capturing these timid and extremely elusive little antelope.

Habitat: In the Park suni inhabit dense deciduous thickets on deep sandy soils. Their very low densities in this habitat tend to indicate that it is largely marginal with more optimal habitat conditions being represented by the closed canopy, dry deciduous woodlands or forests further eastwards.

Habits: Even in their choice habitats suni are seldom seen owing to their secretive habits, and consequently very little is known of them. At the first sign of danger they crouch down in some suitable cover and "freeze", and will only dart off to the nearest alternative cover if the threat persists. Suni apparently form stable pair-bonds, the pair often being accompanied by the young while still in the immature stages. There are strong indications that they are territorial, or at least occupy the same home ranges for long periods at a time. They also have the habit of using communal dung-heaps.

Suni are usually confined to areas of dense undergrowth. They do, however, occasionally wander into clearings for feeding purposes.

Owing to their secretive habits and the forest/thicket habitats they occupy, suni are most commonly preyed upon by leopard, python and large forest-dwelling eagles such as the crowned eagle.

Only male suni have horns and males and females are similar in size. Adults attain a body mass of five kilograms and the life-span is between six and 10 years.

Diet: The available records indicate that suni are probably exclusively browsers.

Breeding: Very little is known of their reproduction and associated behaviour. Casual observations suggest that the young are born during early summer.

Suni

Impala

Aepyceros melampus

Rooibok

Distribution: Impala are the most abundant of the antelope species in the Park and occur widespread throughout the area. The largest concentrations are found along the perennial rivers, or other sources of permanent water. They are particularly numerous in the area between the Crocodile and Olifants rivers with notable concentrations along the Crocodile, Sabie, Sand and Olifants rivers, as well as along the Nwaswitsontso, Sweni, Nwanetsi and Timbavati rivers in the region of Tshokwane, Satara, Nwanetsi and Orpen. North of the Olifants River they are common along the Letaba, Shingwedzi, Phugwane, Mphongolo and Luvuvhu rivers.

Habitat: Despite their abundance and wide distribution, impala have distinct habitat preferences, which are shown clearly by their heavy concentrations in selected areas. The most important features of optimal impala habitat are a perennial water supply, and short grass or trampled areas with forbs and medium or dense stands of shrubs. Though impala are dependent on a regular supply of water they in fact prefer the vegetation of semi-arid areas. They avoid tall grass areas, which accounts for their low numbers in the Pretoriuskop area and almost total absence from the rank stands of medium to tall grass on the eastern plains north of the Letaba River.

Habits: Impala are highly gregarious animals and under optimal habitat conditions form herds numbering several hundreds. However, herds are generally much smaller and the largest proportion of the population consists of herds ranging in size from 10 to 60 animals.

Herd composition alters as the year progresses to coincide with the different phases of the breeding cycle. The rut, or mating season, commences in April and lasts until June. During this period the adult rams establish territories and each ram attempts to confine a group of females and their young to his territory. Only one adult male therefore accompanies each female herd. All yearling males are evicted from the female groups and form bachelor groups that linger on the peripheries of the territories. A great amount of activity is obvious amongst the territorial males, which constantly have to defend their boundaries from intrusion by adjacent males or challenges from the more dominant of the bachelors. In addition, each territorial male has to contend with the "herding" of females to retain them within his domain as the ewes do not acknowledge the territorial boundaries and move from one territory to the next.

Impala ewe

Impala rams

In the defence of their territories the males resort to elaborate displays. Typically the defending males will approach rivals with the tail outstretched and the hairs fanned out laterally to reveal the conspicuous white undersurface and with the nose extended forward; at the same time they utter awesome guttural snorts. When the rut reaches its peak these snorts may be heard continuously throughout the day and night in impala habitat. If displaying is not sufficient to discourage rivals, fighting will ensue. During these encounters the males lunge forward and engage in fierce pushing duels. Frequently the males become so preoccupied when fighting that they pay little or no attention to potential sources of danger and may be approached to within a metre or two before taking flight. After the rut, peace and calm returns to the population. Though some bachelor males remain segregated from the herds others join the female groups.

By virtue of their numbers impala make an important contribution to the diet of all the larger predators. They are preyed upon by hyaena, wild dog, cheetah, leopard, lion, crocodile and, in the case of juveniles, by jackal, baboons, pythons and martial eagles.

Impala are sociable animals and are often encountered in the company of other species, for example baboons, zebra, wildebeest, giraffe and kudu. During the lambing season, however, impala avoid the company of baboons, most likely because of the latter's habit of preying upon the young lambs.

Only male impala have horns and they are slightly larger than the females. Adults can weigh up to 50 kilograms and have a life-span of 12 to 15 years.

Diet: Impala are largely catholic in their choice of food, being both browsers and grazers and feeding on a wide range of food plants. They are particularly well adapted to disturbed (that is heavily utilised and trampled) areas where they feed on grasses and forbs, or on the leaves, flowers and seed-pods of shrubs and trees. Impala are therefore adapted to maintain healthy populations and high densities in areas where many other species would find it difficult to survive.

Breeding: The well-defined lambing season stretches from mid-October to mid-December. Some impala ewes have their first lamb at two years of age though the majority lamb for the first time in their third year. The gestation period is seven months. Though twins have been recorded, they are exceptional. Young lambs do not go through a period of concealment following birth but are strong and agile enough to follow their dams within a few hours.

Grey rhebok

Grey rhebok *Pelea capreolus*

Vaalribbok

Distribution: Grey rhebok occur on several of the high mountain plateaux to the immediate south of the Park in the Malelane area. As circumstantial evidence exists that they may once have occurred within the Park, a number were introduced to the plateau of the Khandizwe Mountain at Malelane a few years ago.
Habitat: High grass-covered mountain plateaux and slopes are the preferred habitat of the grey rhebok. They favour areas with a sparse cover of woody plants and a well-developed grass stand.
Habits: Grey rhebok are semi-gregarious and associate in small groups, numbering up to 10 or 12 individuals. As they are territorial, each group is accompanied by a single harem or group male. Young males are evicted from the breeding groups and lead a solitary life until they are able to acquire their own females.

Territorial demarcation is accomplished by ritualised posturing and vocalisations. It is probable that some form of scent-mark is also used.

Only male grey rhebok possess horns and the sexes are similar in size. Adults attain a body mass of around 20 kilograms and have a life-span of around 10 years.
Diet: Grey rhebok appear to be exclusively grazers though little information is available on their food preferences.
Breeding: A single lamb is born during a well-defined lambing season in late spring and early summer. The gestation period is approximately eight months. Following birth the lamb remains concealed for some time before joining the group.

Roan antelope *Hippotragus equinus*

Bastergemsbok

Distribution: The major concentration of the Park's roan antelope population is on the basalt plains adjoining the Lebombo Mountains in the eastern half of the Park, north of the Letaba River. Scattered herds also occur in the more heavily wooded savanna in the adjacent western side of the Park. A small relict population, the last vestige of a once wide-ranging population in the undulating foothills of the Drakensberg Mountains between Pretoriuskop and White River, still persists in the region to the south of Pretoriuskop. Two small subpopulations which existed north of the Orpen Rest Camp and along the eastern boundary to the north-east of Mlondozi Dam, have become extinct in recent years.

Habitat: Roan antelope are characteristically found in lightly wooded savanna with a well-developed field layer of medium to tall (between 0,5 and 1,5 metres high) grasses. The condition of the field layer plays a vital rôle in their choice of habitat and they largely avoid overgrazed and short grass areas. Where they occur in more densely wooded habitats roan will be found in the lower-lying areas which normally have fewer shrubs and trees and a better developed grass layer.

Habits: Roan antelope are semi-gregarious and normally associate in herds ranging from five to twelve animals. Larger herds of up to 25 individuals are also occasionally found. Each herd is accompanied by a single mature bull only, immature bulls being evicted from the breeding herds in their third year usually at an age of 26 to 30 months. A dominance hierarchy exists amongst the females, with the most dominant female being the leader of the herd. Female calves remain in the herd. As the herd increases in size subgroups form amongst the cows and their offspring. These subgroups form the nuclei for new herds when the herd becomes too large.

Each breeding herd occupies its own home range. These home ranges include favoured wet and dry season areas and may be 60 to 100 square kilometres in size. Though home ranges are largely exclusive to each roan herd, some overlap between adjoining herds occasionally occurs. This system of largely non-overlapping home ranges, together with the roan antelope's semi-gregarious social system and its predilection for particular habitats, contributes to its sparse distribution in the Park. Another factor is the extreme susceptibility of this species to the lethal enzootic disease anthrax.

Once young males have been evicted from the herds they form "bachelor groups", usually consisting of two to four individuals but sometimes numbering eight or more. A dominance hierarchy also exists amongst these males and the most dominant becomes the contender for a breeding group.

Herd bulls fend off challenges for their herd by means of a series of ritualised displays. During these displays the postures of the head, ears and tail are of particular significance – in both the dominant and subordinate animals. Where threat displays do not succeed in dissuading rivals, fierce fighting may ensue. In these ritualised contests, fighting consists of an intensive pushing duel with both contestants on their knees. The one to push the other off the mark is the victor and the fighting is not intended to cause bodily harm. However, when confronted by carnivores, or when wounded, roan antelope are known to be pugnacious fighters and their scimitar-shaped horns have often proved lethal weapons to an unwary foe.

Roan antelope

A week or two before parturition a roan cow will leave the herd and withdraw to a secluded area to await the birth. For the first six weeks of life the reddish-brown calf conceals itself in a clump of tall grass or other suitable cover for most of the day while the mother rejoins the herd. During daylight the only contact between mother and calf is during the early morning. Calves of similar age form very close ties, which remain intact into adulthood in the case of females.

By virtue of their size and pugnacious disposition adult roan antelope have few enemies and are only vulnerable to predation by lion. The young and subadults are, however, also preyed upon by leopard, cheetah, spotted hyaena and wild dog.

Both male and female roan antelope possess horns, but those of the males are heavier than those of the females. The male roan is also heavier and stouter than the female. Adults attain a body mass of about 270 kilograms and have a life-span of 12 to 15 years.

Diet: Roan antelope are primarily grazers, but occasionally browse when grasses are mature and dry. Under optimal conditions they do not normally feed below around 8 to 10 centimetres above the ground, hence – among other reasons – their partiality for medium to tall grass.

Breeding: Roan antelope cows have their first calf at the age of three years and are prolific breeders, calving once every 10 or 11 months. The gestation period is nine months, and three to six weeks after giving birth the roan cow normally conceives again. Calves are born throughout the year with no definite calving peaks. No confirmed cases of twins are known.

Sable *Hippotragus niger*

Swartwitpens

Distribution: Though densities vary, sable antelope occur almost throughout the Park, the only notable exception being the extreme south-eastern corner between Lower Sabie and Crocodile Bridge. Their major concentrations are in the Pretoriuskop region, the Manzimhlope area on the Hlangulene road, the Phalaborwa Gate area and along the western half of the Park north of the Letaba River.

Habitat: As with its cousin the roan antelope, the sable antelope is also partial to areas with a well-developed field layer, with medium to tall grasses (about half a metre to one and a half metres in height). Sable are, however, ecologically separated from roan by their distinct preference for well-drained, sandy soils and the accompanying higher density of trees and shrubs. The highest densities of sable in the Park are therefore found in the western and south-western areas with granitic, sandy soils and relatively dense savanna woodland.

Habits: Sable antelope are gregarious animals and associate in herds ranging in size from a few individuals to 40 or more. The overall average herd size in the Park is 14. In social organisation and habits they closely resemble the roan antelope.

Breeding herds are accompanied by a single herd bull with immature males being forcibly evicted by the herd bull in their third year. Female calves remain with the herd. Although the herd bull is dominant over the cows, the leadership of the herd is assumed by the most dominant cow. The cohesion between sable herd members is considerably greater than in roan antelope.

Nursery herds occupy home ranges which are notably smaller than those of

Sable bull

the roan antelope and are about 200 to 400 hectares in extent. These home ranges are largely exclusive and there is little overlap with adjoining herds. Although sable antelope reach higher densities in their favoured habitats than roan antelope – because of their smaller home ranges and larger herds – they may nevertheless also be considered a low-density species.

As the young males are driven from the breeding herds they gather together to form "bachelor groups", which number from two to three up to as many as 10, but very rarely more. The social order in these groups is determined by a dominance hierarchy which is maintained by frequent ritualised displays; in these, the posture of the head, ears and tail is especially important, as in the roan antelope. Young males remain in the bachelor groups for two to three years before they can contend for their own breeding herd by attempting to evict a reigning herd bull.

Herd bulls retain sole rights over a breeding herd by fighting off challengers. When a bull is challenged, threat behaviour initially consists of a series of ritualised displays in which the bulls take an upright stance, with the head held high, the ears outstretched and the tail extended from the body. Mere posturing can force a bull of low social standing into submission but if the two contenders are evenly matched and the challenge continues, the bulls fall on to their knees, clash their horns and the fighting develops into a fierce pushing duel before the weaker of the two jumps up and beats a hasty retreat. This form of ritualised fighting prevents bodily harm but occasionally results in a horn being broken. When confronted by carnivores, or wounded, sable antelope become extremely aggressive and are pugnacious fighters. They are quite capable of killing the largest of predators.

Prior to giving birth, sable antelope cows leave the breeding herd and withdraw to a secluded area with suitable cover in the form of tall grass or shrubs. For the first two weeks following birth the calves are nursed early in the morning, after which they leave the mother and lie down in a clump of dense grass or under a shrub for the rest of the day. For the first two to three days the mother remains within a few hundred metres of her calf but later moves progressively further away and rejoins the herd. After the initial two weeks the calves become more active and form cohesive nursery groups. At this stage they will seek the company of the mother only to nurse, spending most of their time with other calves in the nurseries. The bonds between female calves remain intact into adulthood.

In contrast to roan antelope, sable appear to be immune to anthrax.

Adult sable antelope attain a body mass of between 230 and 250 kilograms and they have a life-span of some 12 to 15 years. Both sexes have horns, those of the males being heavier than those of the females. The body colour of adult males tends towards black while that of the females remains reddish-brown as in juveniles of both sexes.

Diet: Sable are almost exclusively grazers, and any intake of browse or forbs appears to be incidental. They normally feed on grass leaves higher than about eight centimetres from the ground under optimal conditions.

Breeding: Sable antelope are strictly seasonal breeders. The rutting season commences towards the end of May and reaches its peak in June and July. After a gestation period of eight months the calves, reddish-fawn in colour, are born in February and March. Out-of-season calves may be born as late as June or July, but are exceptional. Twins have not been recorded. Cows give birth for the first time at the age of three years.

Buffalo *Syncerus caffer*

Buffel

Distribution: Buffalo herds are generally and widely distributed throughout the Kruger National Park.

Habitat: Buffalo are extremely adaptable animals and occupy all the habitats represented in the Park. They are as well suited to habitats of open grassland as they are to more heavily wooded savanna, to woodlands and even to thickets. In their choice of habitat the length of the grass apparently plays a minor rôle as they occur in both tall and short grass areas and are also capable of utilising heavily grazed and trampled areas. Topographically buffalo are equally at home on gently undulating plains and in rugged, mountainous areas where they only appear to avoid the steeper slopes. Old bulls separated from the breeding herds are partial to thickets or reed-beds in the neighbourhood of perennial water.

Habits: Buffalo are highly gregarious animals and associate in herds of up to 1 000 individuals or more. In Central and East Africa herds of up to 3 000 have been reported. However, the average herd size in the Park is 300.

Buffalo herds inhabit established home ranges for prolonged periods. These home ranges include winter (dry season) concentration and summer (wet season) dispersal areas. Buffalo are not territorial and there is consequently considerable overlap in the home ranges of adjoining herds. In times of adverse environmental conditions, buffalo herds will leave their normal home ranges in search of more favourable conditions, often splitting up into smaller groups of a few to several dozen individuals.

Despite their size and their well-deserved reputation as the most dangerous of adversaries when wounded or cornered, buffalo are extremely peaceful towards one another. Social status and the harmony between individuals is achieved through a dominance hierarchy which is largely determined by age. The hierarchical position of an individual is also important in determining mating priorities. However, mating is not restricted to the most dominant bull only, but is performed by several of the senior bulls.

Subadult bulls are not forcibly evicted from the breeding herds as in several of the antelope species, but voluntarily leave and rejoin the herds. Old bulls eventually become permanently separated from the breeding herds and linger on as singletons or in bachelor groups of from two or three individuals to as many as 30 (and occasionally even more).

Lion and large crocodiles are the only predators capable of preying upon adult buffalo. In fact, buffalo are a favoured prey species of lion and prides are frequently encountered on the outskirts of large buffalo herds. During aerial censusing of buffalo, park biologists have witnessed several cases where lion have opportunistically stalked buffalo while the latter were flustered by the noise of the census helicopter. Numerous cases are also on record where only the concerted efforts of a number of lions over several hours have resulted in the overwhelming and killing of a buffalo bull.

By virtue of their mass and the size of their herds buffalo can exert a profound influence on their environment. Ecologically, they fulfil the important function of reducing rank and tall grass stands to a more open and shorter state, which makes the habitat more acceptable to a number of associated herbivores. However, during adverse conditions, such as a prolonged drought, their impact on the water and food resources may be severe. When drinking, buffalo have the habit of entering the water waist-deep. During droughts this habit causes considerable churning and turns the available water into a muddy suspension, which can have the effect of preventing other animals from drinking from the same source.

Both sexes have horns but those of the bulls are heavier and more robust than those of the cows. Bulls are also more massive than cows and can attain a mass of up to 800 kilograms (females up to 750 kilograms). They have a lifespan of 15 to 20 years.

Diet: Though they are almost exclusively grazers, buffalo have no other apparent preferences regarding their food resource. They readily feed on tall coarse grasses and play an important rôle in opening up dense grass stands for species preferring short grass conditions. Buffalo are, however, also capable of feeding on short grass. They are dependent on a regular water supply, which is used for drinking and wallowing.

Breeding: The calving season extends over a period of several months, with a peak from March to May. The gestation period is just over 11 months and cows calve for the first time at five to six years of age. The cows do not leave the herd when giving birth and within a few hours the calf is strong enough to keep up with its mother and the herd.

Buffalo

Kudu

Tragelaphus strepsiceros

Koedoe

Distribution: The kudu is the most widely distributed antelope species in the Park, and inhabits, albeit in varying densities, all the habitats represented in the area.

Habitat: The wide distribution of the kudu reflects its ability to adapt to a wide range of habitats. On the eastern plains north of the Letaba River, its densities are lower than in most other habitats largely because of the almost homogeneous stands of mopane shrubs which occur there: mopane is not a favoured food-plant of the kudu. It is also well suited to rugged, broken country and is partial to hilly and mountainous terrain.

Habits: Kudu are semi-gregarious animals which associate in small family groups consisting on average of five to seven animals. Larger herds numbering 12 to 14 are not uncommon and on occasion herds of up to 25 can be encountered. They are not known to establish and defend territories though the herds occupy the same home range for several years.

Adult bulls leave the breeding herds for most of the year and form bachelor groups. Separation of the bulls from the breeding herds appears to be voluntary as they are not evicted by a more dominant herd bull. Aggression amongst bulls, which is infrequent in comparison with most other antelope species, appears to serve the sole function of establishing and maintaining a dominance hierarchy.

In common with other antelope, such aggressive encounters as do occur amongst kudu bulls consist of ritualised displays or severe pushing duels where the strength of the contestants is tested without the intention of doing bodily harm. However, a number of cases are on record where the long spiral horns have become interlocked during severe skirmishes. Unable to disengage and therefore prohibited from moving about freely the contestants either fall easy prey to predators or eventually die of thirst and starvation.

Being dependent on browse for the bulk of their diet, kudu are vulnerable

Kudu cow

Kudu bulls

in prolonged droughts when deciduous trees and shrubs shed their leaves early in the dry season and they are exposed to a period of acute food shortage before the onset of the spring rains. However, when deciduous plants retain their leaves well into the dry season during periods of high rainfall, kudu populations are capable of responding quite dramatically and soon regain their numbers. Fluctuations in the Park's kudu populations are often therefore directly correlated with rainfall patterns. They are also, however, extremely vulnerable to anthrax enzootics.

Their major predators are lion, while subadults are also preyed upon by leopard, cheetah, spotted hyaena, wild dog, and crocodile.

Only male kudu have horns and they are considerably larger than the females in body size; males attain a mass of around 250 kilograms while females on average attain 160 kilograms. The life-span of a kudu is between 12 and 15 years.

Diet: Kudu are primarily browsers though they do occasionally graze. At the end of a dry spell when most deciduous trees and shrubs have shed their leaves, they readily take the young green forbs which are the first to sprout in spring. They are also attracted to burned areas where they feed heavily on the forbs which sprout after a fire.

Breeding: Though there is a peak in calf births during March and April, the rutting and calving seasons are ill-defined and extend over several months. A single calf of a reddish-fawn colour is born after a gestation period of seven months. No confirmed cases of twins have been recorded and cows calve for the first time at three years of age. For the first three weeks after birth, calves are attended intermittently by their mothers for short periods only, remaining concealed for most of the time in suitable cover such as tall grass or shrubs.

Nyala

Tragelaphus angasii

Njala

Distribution: Nyala are common in the riparian vegetation of the Luvuvhu and Limpopo rivers. They are also found in fairly high densities in the broken, mountainous terrain to the north of Punda Maria, in the Nyandu Sandveld south of Pafuri and along the Shingwedzi River, especially east of the Shingwedzi Rest Camp. Smaller widely scattered groups are, however, also found throughout the area north of the Olifants River. Stragglers are occasionally also reported from the Tshokwane/Orpen Dam area. A small population of nyala has also been successfully established along the Sabie River.

Habitat: The highest densities of nyala are found in riparian woodlands or forest (closed tree canopies) with a relatively open understorey of shrubs. Though nyala and bushbuck are partial to much the same habitats, nyala are more common than bushbuck where the understorey is less dense, and vice versa. Nyala also occur in drier ravines and in woodlands on hillslopes.

Habits: Nyala are semi-gregarious. Males are commonly encountered singly or in bachelor groups of two or three, and occasionally in groups of as many as five or more. Females and young are most frequently found in small groups of up to five individuals, though these groups too may also be larger. Groups exceeding 12 to 15 animals are rare.

Nyala do not establish territories and there is a free overlap of home ranges between neighbouring individuals or groups. Groups are not stable units and individuals may change freely from one group to another. In contrast to the

Nyala ewe

Nyala ram

closely related bushbuck there is a considerable amount of aggressive interaction between nyala males. These encounters mostly take the form of extremely impressive ritualised displays during which the males circle one another, moving forward in slow, deliberate paces while the knees are lifted high. Simultaneously, the horns are tilted forward, the head is lowered and the ridge of white hair on the back is erected while the tail is also curled upwards to expose the white undersurface. Actual fighting amongst males is not common and consists mainly of pushing duels. Such encounters are believed to serve the function of establishing and maintaining a dominance hierarchy. In species which establish territories, for example the sassaby, the proprietor of a territory has the sole mating rights as long as he can ward off his rivals. Where the territorial system does not exist, as with the nyala and the buffalo, mating priorities are determined by the male's position in the dominance hierarchy.

Nyala are preyed upon by lion, leopard, crocodile, spotted hyaena and wild dog.

Only male nyala have horns. They are also conspicuously larger in body size than females and attain a mass of 100 to 125 kilograms compared with the females' 55 to 68 kilograms. Females are chestnut in colour with short hair while the males are slate-grey to dark brown to black in colour with a coat of long hair. They have a life-span of 15 years.

Diet: The diet of the nyala varies seasonally, depending on the availability of preferred food plants, but averaged over the year consists of roughly equal proportions of grass and browse.

Breeding: Births occur throughout the year though there are indications of a higher rate of births for the period August to April. Ewes give birth for the first time at the age of two years and the gestation period is just over seven months. Usually only one lamb is born though twins have been recorded. Young calves remain concealed for their first two weeks after which they become more active and follow their mothers.

Bushbuck

Tragelaphus scriptus

Bosbok

Distribution: Bushbuck are widespread throughout the Park but occur patchily because they are restricted to riparian vegetation and similarly dense habitat in valleys and on hillslopes. Their major concentrations are found in the riverine forests along the Sabie, Luvuvhu and Limpopo rivers and in the well-wooded parts of the Punda Maria and Pretoriuskop sections.

Habitat: They are largely retricted to the dense riparian vegetation and reed-beds of the major watercourses, but also inhabit hillslopes and valleys with relatively dense savanna vegetation or woodlands.

Habits: Bushbuck are primarily solitary animals, but also form small family groups consisting of a mother and her infant, or loose associations of a male and female or even two or three males together. The associations are of a temporary nature and often only last a few hours. Adult animals mix freely and regroupings do not necessarily involve the same individuals. Bushbuck are extremely tolerant towards one another and even mild forms of aggression, such as dominance displays which are common in most other antelopes, are exceptional. On the infrequent occasions when they do display, the crest along the back is erected while the back itself is arched and the tail is curved forward over the back. Bushbuck do not establish territories but have favoured areas, or home ranges, to which they confine most of their activities. There is considerable overlap in the home ranges of adjoining individuals. They are essentially nocturnal animals but may often be seen feeding in the early morning, late evening, or during the day in overcast, cool weather.

Though bushbuck are gentle towards one another they are known to be fierce and courageous fighters when wounded or cornered. Many well-trained gun dogs, and even leopards (the bushbuck's major predator), have beaten a hasty retreat in encounters with enraged rams.

Only male bushbuck have horns. The sexes differ in colour, males being dark brown in contrast to the light brown or chestnut-brown of the females. Males attain a mass of 30 to 50 kilograms and females are lighter at 24 to 34 kilograms. The life-span of the bushbuck is around 10 to 12 years.

Bushbuck ewe

Bushbuck ram

Diet: The bulk of the bushbuck's diet consists of browse, though grasses may contribute up to a third of the total intake.
Breeding: There is no well-defined lambing season though there is a peak in the number of births during October and November. A ewe will have her first lamb at just under two years of age. The gestation period is six months and no confirmed cases of twins have been recorded. Lambs remain concealed for the first few weeks following birth before they are strong enough to move around with their mothers.

Eland *Taurotragus oryx*

Eland

Distribution: Eland occur widely scattered north of the Olifants River, with the highest densities in the more heavily wooded savannas along the western half of the Park, the eastern open plains north of the Shingwedzi River and in the sandveld areas and floodplains between the Luvuvhu and Limpopo rivers. South of the Olifants River all the natural populations were extirpated before the inception of the Park. Attempts are now under way to re-establish a population in the Pretoriuskop area, while a few eland which escaped after similar reintroduction exercises in the private nature reserves to the west of the Park have settled in the area to the north-west of Satara.
Habitat: Eland do not exhibit any specific habitat preferences but occupy a wide range of savanna habitats.
Habits: They are gregarious animals and may be encountered in herds of 100 or more, though the average herd sizes range between five and 15. During the winter months the herds frequently split and regroup, while in the summer they appear to be more stable. Though eland are known to be highly mobile animals and capable of moving over long distances, their annual routine in the Park largely conforms to a stable pattern. Movements within their established ranges are apparently largely prompted by environmental considerations and are not necessarily associated with cyclic migration patterns.

Old bulls are often encountered on their own or in small groups of two or three. The reason for the segregation of these bulls from the breeding herds is not clear as young males are not evicted forcibly from the herds and a number of adult bulls normally accompany the breeding herds.

Eland bull

Reedbuck ram

Reedbuck ewe

Despite their great size eland are spectacular jumpers; they can clear two-metre-high game fences with ease and, while trotting, individuals often take great leaps into the air in wild abandon – on occasion even jumping over one another – for no apparent reason.

Prior to giving birth eland cows leave the herd and withdraw to a secluded area. Shortly after birth the young calf conceals itself in suitable cover and remains hidden for the first week or two while the mother remains with it. Two or three cows frequently group together during this period before re-joining the main herd.

Lion are the only predators capable of preying on an adult eland though subadults are taken by leopard, cheetah, spotted hyaena and wild dog.

The sexes are similar although the horns of the bulls are stouter than those of the cows and the bulls are larger in body size. Old bulls also tend to turn blue-grey and are then conspicuously different from the fawn-coloured cows. Males may attain a mass of 700 kilograms while females are smaller at up to 460 kilograms. Their life-span is approximately 15 years.

Diet: Eland take mostly browse, including forbs, though they may also feed on grass to some extent.

Breeding: A single fawn-coloured calf, slightly more reddish than the adult in colour, is born after a gestation period of nine months. Although there is a calving peak from September to November calves may be born throughout the year. Eland cows calve for the first time at the age of three years.

Reedbuck *Redunca arundinum*

Rietbok

Distribution: The reedbuck is patchily distributed and locally abundant in suitable habitats throughout the Park. It occurs in high densities in the tall-grass areas of the south-western regions between Pretoriuskop and Malelane and in the Nshawu Valley, north of Letaba.

Habitat: As its name implies, the reedbuck is most commonly found in the neighbourhood of vleis or marshy areas. The most important component of reedbuck habitat appears to be a well-developed tall-grass layer around 1,5 metres high, especially in the vicinity of watercourses.

Habits: Reedbuck are semi-gregarious, and occur singly, in pairs or small family groups of three or four. Though the male is dominant over the female, the female initiates movements to and from the grazing sites and watering points and therefore acts as leader of the group. Reedbuck males establish territories which are defended against intrusion by other reedbuck males. These territories normally range from 35 to 60 hectares in size. In encounters between males aggression takes the form of highly ritualised displays which include various postures aimed at intimidating the opponent into submission. If this does not succeed the males lock their horns, lower their heads and engage in a fierce pushing duel until one jumps up and runs away. As in most antelopes, therefore, fighting is merely a test of strength and is not intended to do bodily harm.

Reedbuck are mostly active during the early morning and late afternoon. In summer they may become more nocturnal in habit. During the day they retire to some suitable tall grass cover. If approached they remain crouched, relying heavily on their cryptic colouration and immobility to escape attention. When flushed, they give a loud whistle as alarm and run away in a series of leaps with the conspicuous white undersurface of the bushy tail turned upwards.

Only male reedbuck have horns. The ram is slightly larger than the ewe and may attain a mass of about 50 to 70 kilograms; the ewe has a mass of between 30 and 50 kilograms. The life-span is around 10 to 12 years.

Diet: Reedbuck feed mainly on grasses and forbs, and only incidentally browse on the leaves of shrubs. Though they will spend some time feeding on the short green flush of grass following a burn, reedbuck are less attracted to such areas than other grazing species and spend most of their time in the tall grass where they find both food and cover.

Breeding: There are indications of a lambing peak from December to May, though births have been recorded throughout the year. Ewes give birth to a single lamb after a gestation period of 7,5 months. Prior to giving birth the ewe isolates herself from the rest of the group. For the first two months following birth the young lamb remains concealed for most of the day and is only attended by the mother during the early morning.

Mountain reedbuck *Redunca fulvorufula*

Rooiribbok

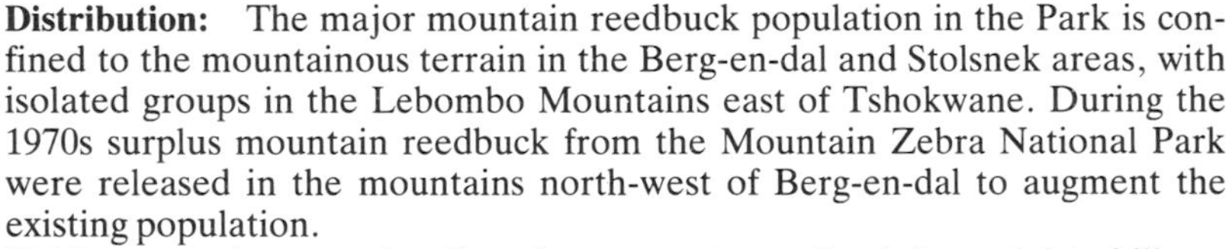

Distribution: The major mountain reedbuck population in the Park is confined to the mountainous terrain in the Berg-en-dal and Stolsnek areas, with isolated groups in the Lebombo Mountains east of Tshokwane. During the 1970s surplus mountain reedbuck from the Mountain Zebra National Park were released in the mountains north-west of Berg-en-dal to augment the existing population.

Habitat: As its name implies, the mountain reedbuck is partial to hilly or mountainous terrain and avoids open plains. Its favoured habitats in the Park are characterised by open savanna vegetation with a well-developed grass layer.

Habits: The normal herd sizes for this semi-gregarious species range from three to six individuals, though as many as 15 or even more may be encountered. Adult mountain reedbuck rams establish territories which are defended against intrusion by other adult males. The breeding herds, consisting of the females and their offspring, are not confined to the territory of any particular male but move from one territory to the next. Young males are

Mountain reedbuck ram and ewe

evicted from the breeding herds by the territorial males. The evicted males either lead a solitary existence or form small bachelor groups until they are capable of establishing their own territories.

As in the reedbuck, the alarm call of the mountain reedbuck is a loud whistle. If pursued, they flee in leaps and bounds – aptly described as a "rocking-horse" action – while the tail is curled forward over the back to expose the conspicuous white undersurface.

In their mountain retreats they are mostly preyed upon by leopards, the other large predators preferring lower-lying terrain.

Only male mountain reedbuck have horns. The males are larger than the females and attain a mass of about 30 kilograms; the females, on average, are about two kilograms lighter. They have a life-span of 10 to 12 years.

Diet: The mountain reedbuck's diet consists almost exclusively of grass. It is also particularly partial to the tender young regrowth in burned areas.

Breeding: Mountain reedbuck have an extended lambing season which coincides with the rainy season, that is, from September to March. Ewes have their first lambs at two years of age. A single lamb is born after a gestation period of seven to eight months. The lamb remains concealed for the first few weeks, after which it joins its mother. During this initial period the lambs are only attended by their mothers for nursing and remain alone and isolated in some suitable cover for most of the time.

Waterbuck *Kobus ellipsiprymnus*

Waterbok

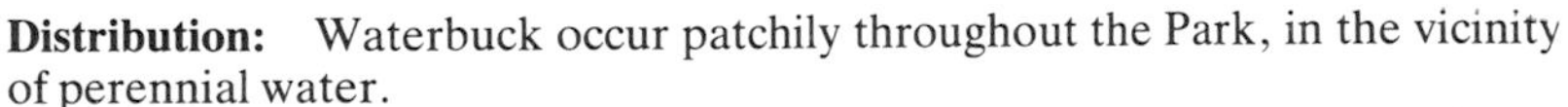

Distribution: Waterbuck occur patchily throughout the Park, in the vicinity of perennial water.

Habitat: In spite of their preference for habitats in the close proximity of perennial water, waterbuck do not favour dense riparian thickets or woodland, but are more partial to savanna habitats with medium to tall grasses between one and one and a half metres high, interspersed with tree and shrub thickets. They are also frequently found in broken, hilly country and even in mountainous areas.

Habits: Waterbuck are gregarious animals and herds of up to 60, but rarely more, may be encountered. However, they are most frequently found in herds ranging in size from 10 to 30 individuals. In the adult age-classes there

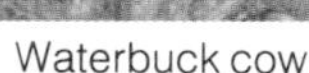

Waterbuck cow Waterbuck bull

is a separation of the sexes with males being evicted from the breeding herds in their second year. These evicted males group together to form bachelor groups. Though waterbuck have been reported to establish territories in studies conducted elsewhere in Africa, evidence of the existence of such a system in the Park is still inconclusive.

During the dry winter months waterbuck spend much of their time grazing along the banks or in the dry beds of the larger perennial rivers. The broad sandy beaches of the Letaba and Olifants rivers, interspersed with reeds and grasses, are especially favoured habitats and during the dry season numerous herds may be seen in these places. During the rainy season waterbuck are more inclined to move further afield and may be seen many kilometres from their winter haunts. Waterbuck wade freely into shallow water and have been reported to take refuge in deeper water when pursued by predators. However, they do not otherwise seem to have particular affinity for swimming or wallowing in water.

Waterbuck are a select item in the diet of lions, and are also preyed upon by leopard, cheetah, spotted hyaena and wild dog in the subadult stages. One of the hazards of leading a riparian existence is predation by crocodiles, and in fact waterbuck are occasionally taken by these reptiles.

Only male waterbuck have horns. The males are larger than the females and may attain a mass of between 250 and 270 kilograms. They have a lifespan of some 14 to 16 years.

Diet: Waterbuck are primarily grazers, but may also browse on forbs and shrubs.

Breeding: Though calves may be born throughout the year, there is a calving peak from January to March. Waterbuck cows give birth for the first time at three years of age and no confirmed cases of twins have been recorded. The fawn-coloured calves remain concealed for two to three weeks, after which they become more active and form "nursery" groups in the herds.

ORDER
PHOLIDOTA

Family
Manidae

Pangolins

Pangolin *Manis temminckii*

Ietermagog

Distribution: Although seldom seen abroad, these shy and peculiar mammals are widespread through the Park wherever termitaria occur.
Habitat: The pangolin appears to have a wide habitat tolerance, occurring on floodplain grasslands, and in savannas and woodlands, but absent from forests.
Habits: Pangolins are mainly nocturnal, but may also be seen during the day, particularly during the early morning. They take refuge in holes or in other secluded places. These animals walk on their back legs only, with the tail raised and the front feet only occasionally touching the ground. They also have a habit of standing up on their hindlegs to look around. If danger threatens they freeze into immobility or roll themselves into a tight ball with the heavy scales on the back and tail completely protecting their soft underparts. If interfered with in this position they may attempt to injure their attacker by scything the tail across the body. Unlike the aardvark they do not have teeth but instead possess a strong, muscular stomach which grinds up the food with the help of gravel they swallow when feeding. The life-span is about 12 years and a mass of eight kilograms or more is attained by adults.
Diet: Pangolins eat ants and occasionally termites which they dig from their nests with the strong claws of the front feet or scratch out from amongst detritus, dead wood or under animal droppings. Their sense of smell is important in locating food and only certain species of termites and ants are favoured.
Breeding: A single young is born after a gestation period of around 139 days. A female carrying its new-born young on the base of its tail has been recorded near Tshokwane during January.

Pangolin

ORDER
RODENTIA

Family
Sciuridae

Squirrels

Tree squirrel

Tree squirrel

Paraxerus cepapi

Boomeekhoring

Distribution: Without doubt the tree squirrel is one of the commonest and most widespread of all small mammal species in the Kruger Park and it may be encountered in diverse ecological conditions and habitats – even in the dense *nsimbitsi* forests of the northern sandveld regions. One would perhaps also expect to find the related red squirrel, *P. palliatus*, to occur in these forests, judging from the proximity of locality records in Mozambique at Chicualacuala just to the north of the Limpopo. As yet, however, no evidence of the occurrence of red squirrels within the Park boundaries has come to light.
Habitat: It is widespread in a wide variety of savanna woodland and dry forest habitats and is particularly common in mopane woodland and forests.
Habits: Tree squirrels are strictly diurnal and although they are arboreal they also feed on the ground. They occur singly, in pairs or in family groups in restricted home ranges and live in holes in trees, where they construct nests of dry leaves. They become exceedingly tame when living close to human habitation and respond readily to being fed. When alarmed they dash for their holes or climb to the top of the nearest tree, where they will hide behind clusters of leaves. The alarm call when annoyed is a loud chatter, "*chuck-chuck-chuck*", repeated for long periods and with the tail flicking up and down in a comical manner. The life-span of these animals is about eight years and adults weigh about 500 grams. Cases of albinism have been recorded in the Park, particularly in the area north of the Olifants River.
Diet: They feed on a wide variety of vegetable matter, foraging both on the ground and in trees. Their diet includes wild fruits, seeds and kernels of various kinds, bulbous roots and even grass. They are also known to eat birds' eggs and insects such as beetles and cicadas.
Breeding: Two to three young are born throughout the year (but mainly in summer) and the gestation period is around 55 days.

ORDER RODENTIA

Family Pedetidae

Springhare

Springhare

Pedetes capensis

Springhaas

Distribution: Springhares are not particularly common in the Park and the major area of distribution coincides with a number of sandveld areas north of the Olifants River. South of this river they have been recorded in the Pumbe Sandveld on the eastern boundary, at Kingfisherspruit, Ngirivani and Nsasane, and at the lower Vutome loop west of Tshokwane.

Habitat: Although the springhare is usually confined to areas of sandy soil or sandy alluvium in savannas, the Kingfisherspruit and Nsasane habitats do not fit this category, the substrates here being of doleritic and basaltic origin respectively.

Habits: Springhares live in burrows which they excavate themselves and from which they emerge only after dark to feed. They prefer light sandy soils for ease of digging, and their distribution is thus largely determined by the availability of such soils. They often construct their burrows in such a manner that they have an entrance tunnel with the sand piled up outside, and an exit tunnel with no sand-pile outside. Deserted springhare burrows are often used for breeding or as refuges by other animals such as mongooses and polecats. At night their reflective eyes are a characteristic sight in sandveld habitats when lights are shone on them but they are not as easily blinded by bright headlights as are true hares. Normally they are alert animals with well-developed senses of hearing, sight and smell. When they are disturbed they take off in leaps and bounds with the tail held high to maintain balance. When moving in this manner they appear very much like miniature kangaroos. They are normally silent animals but scream when caught or injured. Their life-span is about eight years and adults attain a mass of 3,5 kilograms.

Diet: Springhares are vegetarian, feeding mainly on the underground stems and rhizomes of grasses; unfortunately, however, they also raid crops and often become a pest in the eyes of the farmer.

Breeding: Single young are born in burrows throughout the year but usually from about November to February. The gestation period is about 45 days.

Springhare

ORDER RODENTIA

Family Hystricidae

Porcupines

Porcupine

Hystrix africaeaustralis

Ystervark

Distribution: The porcupine is a common animal and is widely distributed throughout the Park in all suitable surroundings.

Habitat: It has a wide habitat tolerance and occurs in most vegetation associations from low to high altitudes and from arid to high rainfall areas. It does, however, give preference to areas where there is ample shelter in the form of caves, rock crevices or piles of loose boulders.

Habits: They are very successful animals, despite their large size and conspicuous form. They owe their survival to their habit of moving about and feeding at night, and lying low by day in caves, rock crevices, old aardvark holes or burrows which they dig themselves. They occur singly, in pairs or in small parties occupying a communal warren. Their presence in these places is often betrayed by quills and accumulations of gnawed bones lying about on the ground outside the warren. The defensive coat of quills which they carry is also an important factor contributing to their survival and, although they are often attacked and killed by the larger predators such as lions, leopards and hyaenas, they are capable of giving a good account of themselves and can inflict fearful wounds with their needle-sharp quills. When annoyed or attacked, they stamp loudly with the hindfeet and rattle the bunch of open-ended quills near the tail. They also erect the other quills on the back and run backwards at their tormentors. When the quills are deeply embedded in the mouths and paws of a predator the wounds often become septic and may prove fatal. Quills are not shot out at the enemy, as is commonly believed, but when they are pushed into an attacker they come loose from the porcupine and remain deeply embedded in the aggressor.

Porcupines are favoured as food all over Africa and the meat is very palatable. Their life-span is about eight years and adults may attain a mass of 18 kilograms.

Diet: Porcupines have a mixed vegetarian diet, which includes roots, bulbs, wild fruits, berries, and the bark of trees, as well as cultivated crops such as groundnuts, melons, potatoes and maize. During periods of drought they take to ring-barking trees such as tamboti, wild mango, wild figs and coral-trees, causing extensive damage and often causing the death of the trees. They also gnaw old bones and ivory and have the habit of dragging such material back to their burrows or caves.

Breeding: Mating has been observed in May and from one to three young are born, usually during the autumn and early winter months (April to July). The gestation period is about two months.

Porcupine

Greater cane-rat

Common molerat

ORDER RODENTIA

Family Thryonomyidae

Cane-rats

Greater cane-rat

Thryonomys swinderianus

Grootrietrot

Distribution: Cane-rats inhabit reed-beds or patches of dense, tall grass along river-banks and streams throughout the Park.

Habitat: They favour *Phragmites* reed-beds and tall grass areas bordering perennial rivers and streams as well as marshy areas.

Habits: These large, robust rodents are not rats at all but are more closely related to porcupines. They generally occur singly, in pairs or in family groups, but can be very abundant in their chosen habitats, where they form "runs" in the matted grass and sedges near the water's edge. They are mainly nocturnal, but sometimes feed in the late afternoon and may also be seen on the move during the day. When disturbed they often take to the water and can swim and dive well. Large numbers are flushed from vleis and marshy places by veld fires. They are considered a delicacy wherever they occur in Africa and are hunted with dogs or captured in special funnel-shaped traps. Cases of albinism have been recorded in the Park in the Malelane area. Adult specimens attain a mass of five kilograms or more.

Diet: Cane-rats are vegetarian and their diet includes the fresh young shoots of *Phragmites* reeds and other types of coarse swamp and aquatic grass, sedges and the bark of certain trees. They will also raid crops and can do extensive damage in sugar-cane plantations. In such situations the python is an important natural enemy, helping to keep their numbers in check.

Breeding: Three to four young are born, usually during the months June to December, although there are also birth records for March.

ORDER RODENTIA

Family Bathyergidae

Rodent moles

Common molerat

Cryptomys hottentotus

Knaagdiermol

Distribution: The common molerat is found throughout the Park in suitable habitat. It would seem that two subspecies are found in the Park, and that *C.h. natalensis* is restricted to the area south of the Olifants River where it is particularly abundant in the more sandy soils towards the south and west. A second subspecies, *C.h. hottentotus*, inhabits the rich basaltic soils and sandy substrates of the northern and eastern regions of the Park. The centre of distribution for this subspecies lies mainly north of the Olifants River, although some specimens have also been collected in the Pumbe Sandveld south of the river.

Habitat: This species has a wide habitat tolerance. Although it seems to prefer softer sandy soils, it is found in a diversity of substrates ranging from fine and compacted soils to soils with high gravel content such as are found on mountain slopes. However, the common molerat is absent from heavy clay or the extremely hard soils normally associated with mopane woodlands.
Habits: These fossorial and communal or semi-communal (sometimes solitary) rodents belong to a family which is exclusively African in distribution. They are adapted for a subterranean existence. Unlike the golden moles which are insectivorous, molerats are vegetarians, feeding on roots, tubers and bulbs, the fibre of which is also utilised for nest-building. Occasionally they leave their burrows at night to feed on the leaves of certain low shrubs. Whereas golden moles loosen the soil with their padded noses and strong claws to form their tunnels, molerats break up the substrate with their large protruding incisors, excavating the loose soil to form the characteristic mounds on the surface. They are particularly active in extending their burrow systems after rains when the soil is wet and soft. If these burrows are opened, molerats are quick to investigate and to repair the damage.
Breeding: Breeding takes place predominantly during spring and summer and one to five young are born in underground nesting-chambers.

ORDER
RODENTIA

Family
Muridae

Old World rats, mice and gerbils

Angoni vlei rat *Otomys angoniensis*

Angoni-vleirot

Distribution: The Angoni vlei rat is an inhabitant of swampy areas or reedbeds and has been collected in suitable habitats in both the northern and southern districts of the Park.
Habitat: Although it is generally associated with wet vleis, damp grassland or swampy ground on the fringes of rivers and vleis, the Angoni vlei rat is recorded as moving from these during the wet season into adjacent drier habitat.
Habits: It is mainly diurnal, although some nocturnal activity has been recorded. Depending on population densities, the Angoli vlei rat may be encountered singly, in pairs or in small family units. They typically construct runways amongst the matted vegetation of their habitat, and these are also extensively used by other species such as shrews and striped mice. The runways are typically strewn with short lengths of discarded grass stems. During the breeding season domed nests of shredded vegetation are constructed on raised ground or in grass tussocks above water level.
Breeding: Females give birth to between two and four young during the warmer, wetter months of summer.

Angoni vlei rat

Bushveld gerbil

Giant rat

Bushveld gerbil

Tatera leucogaster

Bosveldnagmuis

Distribution: The bushveld gerbil is a common species throughout the Park, particularly in sandveld areas. Its characteristic burrows are easily detected at the bases of low bushes or shrubs.
Habitat: They favour sandy ground, light soils and areas of alluvium in savannas or grassland with scrub cover. These gerbils do not generally occur in areas of heavy soil, but where they do, they prefer to utilise holes in termitemounds and other such refuges instead of digging their own burrows.
Habits: The bushveld gerbil is a nocturnal species which can be very abundant in certain choice habitats, and in agricultural areas may cause considerable damage to crops.
Breeding: They breed throughout the year (with a peak during the summer months) and the litter size varies from three to seven, with an average of four.

Giant rat

Cricetomys gambianus

Reuserot

Distribution: This species has for many years been rumoured to occur in the eastern foothills of the Soutpansberg to the west of Punda Maria. Recently it has been photographed and collected in the Punda Maria Rest Camp. These records obviously represent the easternmost distribution of an isolated population occurring along the Soutpansberg.
Habitat: This essentially tropical species prefers the evergreen forests and woodlands of the higher rainfall areas where there is adequate undercover; this habitat is found along the southern slopes of the Soutpansberg.
Habits: The giant rat is terrestrial, although in rare instances it will climb trees for fruit if food is scarce on the ground. These docile and slow-moving animals are nocturnal, and normally solitary except when breeding or when a

female is raising a litter. They excavate extensive burrow systems with several chambers, some of which are used to hoard food, others for latrines, as sleeping-chambers, or for raising litters. Burrow systems always have two or more escape tunnels other than the vertical entrance shaft. The entrances are plugged with soil every time the occupant enters its refuge to spend the day. Invariably the floor of the burrow system is strewn with food remains such as pips, kernels and other inedible bits and pieces. Apart from such items, giant rats also hoard a host of other objects such as small stones, pieces of bone, nails, wire, string and similar rubbish.
Breeding: From scattered information it would appear that the giant rat breeds during summer. Two to four hairless young are born per litter after a gestation period of four weeks.

Pouched mouse

Saccostomus campestris

Wangsakmuis

Distribution: The pouched mouse is another rodent inhabitant of woodland and woodland savannas throughout the entire Park, but it is not particularly common anywhere.
Habitat: They are catholic in their habitat requirements, but the preferred habitats of this species are sandy soils or sandy alluvium with scrub bush or open woodland. When occurring on harder ground they make use of the cover of fallen logs, holes in termite-mounds or any other situation that affords shelter.
Habits: The pouched mouse is nocturnal and terrestrial. It is a relatively slow-moving creature and is easy to capture by hand at night. It is not aggressive and can become very tame in captivity. Although it is predominantly a seed-eater it will occasionally feed on insects such as harvester-termites. The seeds of such plants as sickle bush, witrosyntjie, and rough-leaved raisin and others are stored in the specialised cheek-pouches for later consumption. It constructs burrows, where it lives and where food items are hoarded. The resting-chamber of its burrow is littered with the unpalatable remains of its meals.
Diet: Pouched mice are predominantly seed-eaters, although insects are taken on rare occasions. A wide variety of seeds are taken, including grass seeds, but the latter form only a small percentage of its food. It appears to have a predilection for acacia seeds.
Breeding: Breeding takes place in spring and summer and from four to ten young are born after a gestation period of 21 days. The average litter size is six.

Pouched mouse

Grey climbing mouse | Chestnut climbing mouse

Grey climbing mouse

Dendromus melanotis

Grysklimmuis

Distribution: The only records of this species in the Kruger National Park are from Willem Picket near Pretoriuskop, Crocodile Bridge and the Punda Maria and Pafuri areas in the far north.

Habitat: The habitat of choice is grassland, with high grass between one and two metres tall. Although the grey climbing mouse is widely distributed, even in arid areas, there is a tendency for it to be more common in riverine environments.

Habits: Although it does climb about in grass stalks, the grey climbing mouse is mainly terrestrial in habit. Unlike the other species of climbing mice, it lives in burrows although it is not known whether it constructs these itself. However, for breeding purposes the grey climbing mouse reverts to the habit of other *Dendromus* species and fashions ball-shaped grass nests on tall grass stalks or amongst the twigs of low shrubs.

Diet: The grey climbing mouse will take seeds, but it appears to be mainly insectivorous.

Breeding: Gravid females with three foetuses each have been taken in the Park during February. Litter size is normally two to four (with a record of up to seven) and young are born all through the summer.

Chestnut climbing mouse

Dendromus mystacalis

Roeskleur-klimmuis

Distribution: This species is relatively rare in the central district of the Park, but has been collected in areas of tall grassveld in the north and particularly in the Pretoriuskop Section of the southern district.

Habitat: Grassland, with high grass between one and two metres tall is the preferred habitat of the chestnut climbing mouse; *Hyparrhenia* grasses are favoured.

Habits: These tiny nocturnal rodents with their handsome chestnut-coloured coats and dark vertebral stripe are excellent climbers, and during

Fat mouse

Common spiny mouse

the breeding season fashion bird-like nests with grass leaves amongst the tall grass stems of their chosen habitat. The long prehensile tail is used extensively as a support when they climb about among grass stems. However, they are also to some extent terrestrial.
Diet: Seeds and insects.
Breeding: A pregnant female with eight foetuses has been collected in March.

Fat mouse *Steatomys pratensis*
Vetmuis

Distribution: An analysis of the pellets of barn owls has indicated that the fat mouse is highly prized and constitutes an important item of the prey of these nocturnal raptors. Skulls and other remnants of the fat mouse have been found in a considerable number of owl pellets collected throughout the Park, and live specimens have been trapped at Shingwedzi, near Bububu Dam and at Kambana.
Habitat: The habitats of choice are grassland and savannas over sandy soils or sandy alluvium. It is not an easy species to trap and consequently features poorly in collections.
Habits: The popular name of this mouse refers to the large quantities of fat stored in its tissues, particularly under the skin. This fat layer is built up in summer and helps to tide the animal through the dry, cold winter months. Fat mice are nocturnal and terrestrial, and are normally encountered singly, although it appears that pairs will coexist for a time during the breeding season. They construct simple tunnels sloping downwards to a grass-filled underground nesting-chamber.
Diet: Mainly seeds, although insects are also taken.
Breeding: Gravid and lactating females have been taken in spring and summer. Up to 9 young are born per litter but the average appears to be three.

Common spiny mouse *Acomys spinosissimus*
Gewone stekelmuis

Distribution: The common spiny mouse is a rock-dwelling species so far only recorded from Punda Maria and the sandstone ridges north and south of the Luvuvhu River in the extreme north-east of the Park, as well as from a single locality (Maswidzudzu sandstone ridge) near Letaba Rest Camp.

Habitat: It is generally associated with rocky koppies, rocky hillsides, stone walls and ravines, but has occasionally been collected in non-rocky surroundings. It is often associated with Lebombo-ironwood thickets.
Habits: The common spiny mouse is partly nocturnal, but in undisturbed conditions it may also be active during the day. Nests are constructed of soft grass and leaves in crannies and amongst boulders, where a number of individuals may shelter together, as many as nine having been recorded on one occasion.
Diet: It feeds on the seeds of grass and other plants, such as jackal-berry, as well as on insects.
Breeding: Gravid females containing from two to three full-term foetuses have been taken in February, and the available evidence from other regions points to a birth season during the summer months.

Single-striped mouse *Lemniscomys rosalia*

Eenstreepmuis

Distribution: The single-striped mouse is an inhabitant of woodlands and grassy plains throughout the Park.
Habitat: It favours grassland within any type of savanna, where it is dependent on a dense grass cover for protection against predators.
Habits: Diurnal, terrestrial and apparently mostly solitary, the single-striped mouse excavates its burrows at the base of shrub or grass tussocks. Well-worn runs are formed from the burrow entrances to the feeding grounds.
Breeding: A female taken in May was pregnant with four foetuses. The available evidence from elsewhere in the Transvaal, however, suggests that the single-striped mouse is a seasonal breeder with most births in summer.

Water rat *Dasymys incomtus*

Waterrot

Distribution: The water rat is a water-loving species which has to date been recorded only from damp vleis and the banks of watercourses in the tall grassveld of the Pretoriuskop area and around Punda Maria in the far north.
Habitat: As its colloquial name suggests, the water rat is associated with swamps, wet vleis and reed-beds along rivers.
Habits: It is crepuscular in habit, that is, it is active during the twilight hours. It is also, however, diurnal to a certain extent. Its grass nests are

Single-striped mouse

Water rat

Woodland mouse House mouse

constructed in grass tussocks or in depressions in the ground above the waterline. From these nests runways lead to its feeding areas. It is terrestrial and semi-aquatic.
Diet: It is vegetarian, feeding on the succulent stems of aquatic vegetation. Insects are, however, taken on occasion.
Breeding: A female suckling three young has been captured in the Park during April. Elsewhere this species has been shown to breed during summer, with litters ranging in size from two to nine young.

Woodland mouse *Grammomys dolichurus*

Woudmuis

Distribution: A few specimens of the woodland mouse have been collected in the riverine forest at the confluence of the Limpopo and Luvuvhu rivers in the extreme north-east of the Park.
Habitat: It is an inhabitant of montane and riverine forests, as well as thickets in woodlands, quite often near permanent water.
Habits: The woodland mouse is nocturnal, and predominantly arboreal. It constructs large and well-hidden nests of plant materials high up in trees.
Diet: It is purely vegetarian, eating fruit, leaves and green bark.
Breeding: A pregnant female with three foetuses has been collected during September at Pafuri, and there are a few records of reproductive activity during summer from Zimbabwe. It will probably prove to be a summer breeder.

House mouse *Mus musculus*

Huismuis

Distribution: Only a single specimen has so far been collected, at Shangoni rangers' quarters on the western boundary of the Park.
Habitat and habits: The house mouse is an introduced species from Eurasia strictly associated with human habitations where it lives in houses and outbuildings amongst packing-cases, boxes or other suitable cover.
Breeding: No records exist for the Park, but it is a prolific breeder. Females can have their first litters at 40 days old, the gestation period is only 19 days and litter sizes range from one to thirteen. The females breed throughout the year and communal nests are sometimes found.

Pygmy mouse

Mus minutoides

Dwergmuis

Distribution: This attractive little mouse has been collected in a variety of habitats throughout the Park.
Habitat: The pygmy mouse has a wide habitat tolerance, and in places lives commensally with man. It burrows in sandy soil, tends to use holes in termite-mounds and other refuges in areas of hard ground, and also lives under debris, fallen logs and any similar type of cover.
Habits: It is nocturnal and terrestrial. Its refuges may be occupied by a single individual, a pair or a family unit, but it forages individually.
Diet: Its food consists mainly of grass seeds, such as those of *Cynodon dactylon*, *Chloris virgata*, and various species of *Andropogon* and *Setaria*. Grass leaves and insects are taken to a lesser extent.
Breeding: The species breeds during summer. After a gestation period of 19 days, litters of one to seven young are born in nests which are defended by both the male and the female.

Natal multimammate mouse

Mastomys natalensis

Natalse vaalveldmuis

Distribution: The Natal multimammate mouse is probably the most common and widely distributed rodent species in the Park and has been collected from a wide range of habitats throughout the area.
Habitat and habits: The species has a wide habitat tolerance and occurs from sea level to an altitude of at least 1 600 metres. It is absent from semi-desert areas, but elsewhere it occurs in grassland with some scrub cover, savannas and on the fringes of forest. It seems to be very successful in colonising disturbed areas, but if such areas recover, the multimammate mouse is gradually replaced by other rodent species. Like the introduced house mouse, it is a species very much commensal with man. It is common in houses in this part of Africa and occurs in stores, outbuildings, huts and other dwellings, nesting in the thatch or under floors. Unfortunately it has been shown

Pygmy mouse

Natal multimammate mouse

to be an important carrier of several diseases that can be transmitted to humans and livestock. It is nocturnal and terrestrial.
Diet: The Natal multimammate mouse is omnivorous. Under natural conditions it subsists on seeds, fruits and other vegetable matter as well as on insects. It may also be cannibalistic under stress, and in human habitations will cause extensive damage to a wide variety of foodstuffs.
Breeding: The species is a prolific seasonal breeder with births taking place mainly during the summer months. The litter size varies from five to 17 with an average of 11 to 12.

Multimammate mouse *Mastomys coucha*
Vaalveldmuis

Distribution: Recent taxonomic research has revealed that what has always been considered to be the species *M. natalensis* (see previous species), actually consists of two morphologically very similar species, namely *M. natalensis* and *M. coucha*. These two species can at present only be separated on the basis of chromosome characteristics, sperm morphology and electrophoretic analyses of proteins. Employing such laboratory techniques, biologists have recently recorded the presence of *M. coucha* at Satara and at Stangene Dam. This implies that some of the prior records of distribution within the Park of the Natal multimammate mouse, may in fact be of the "ordinary" multimammate mouse. However, as both species appear to be fairly common throughout their respective ranges and since their known ranges of distribution appear to overlap in the Park, it is possible that both occur throughout the whole area. The situation nevertheless requires further clarification.
Habitat and habits: As far as can be ascertained, it is similar to *M. natalensis* in habitat and habits.
Breeding: Apparently its breeding habits are also similar to that of the Natal multimammate mouse.

Multimammate mouse

Tree rat

Tree rat
Thallomys paedulcus

Boomrot

Distribution: The tree rat is an arboreal species which has been collected in suitable localities north of the Sabie River. So far no records have been forthcoming from the southern district.
Habitat: Tree rats are most often found associated with open acacia savannas or woodlands, where their large grass nests are found in umbrella-thorn, tamboti and nyala trees.
Habits: They are nocturnal and almost exclusively arboreal. They construct nests from fine vegetable matter in hollow tree-trunks or under loose bark. Occasionally tree rats will construct a nest in the open on a sturdy branch, rather similar in appearance to a weaver-bird's nest. These nests are occupied by a number of individuals, all of which appear to continue adding building material to the structure.
Diet: They feed on the fine fresh leaflets of acacia trees, and the green outer coating of the seed-pods.
Breeding: No records exist from the Park but elsewhere a summer breeding season is indicated. Two to five young are born per litter.

Red veld rat

Red veld rat
Aethomys chrysophilus

Afrikaanse bosrot

Distribution: The red veld rat is a common rodent species distributed in woodland areas throughout the Park.
Habitat: It is fairly catholic in its habitat requirements, occurring both in grassland and savanna woodland. The species is, however, particularly associated with substantial cover in the form of thick shrubs, clumps of grass, rocks, boulders, piles of debris, fallen logs, holes in termitaria and so on. It occasionally occurs as a commensal with man.
Habits: It is nocturnal and terrestrial and excavates its burrows under the cover of bushes or more substantial cover. It is not gregarious and is found singly, in pairs or as a family group.
Breeding: This is a polyoestrous species which breeds throughout the year, but with a distinct birth peak during summer. One to six young per litter are born in grass-lined nests in the shelters.

Namaqua rock mouse House rat

Namaqua rock mouse

Aethomys namaquensis

Namakwa-klipmuis

Distribution: The Namaqua rock mouse is very common and has been collected in suitable rocky surroundings throughout the Park.
Habitat: It is generally confined to rocky hillsides, ravines and piles of boulders, but in the absence of this type of habitat it will occasionally utilise holes in trees in savanna woodland. The untidy and rather massive grass and twig nests of the Namaqua rock mouse are a conspicuous feature of all the habitats it frequents and live specimens may usually be taken in the vicinity of such nests.
Habits: It is nocturnal, communal, terrestrial, and partly arboreal.
Breeding: Gravid females containing from two to seven foetuses have been taken throughout summer.

House rat

Rattus rattus

Huisrot

Distribution: Like the house mouse, the house rat is another introduced species which has fortunately only been found so far at Skukuza and Pretoriuskop rest camps. Park staff are attempting to eradicate it and prevent it from spreading.
Habitat and habits: The species has a wide habitat tolerance. However, throughout its range it is almost exclusively commensal with man, associated with sheds in which food and grain are stored. It also enters houses and is a destructive pest and a menace to human health.
Breeding: There are no records as yet from the Park. It is, however, known to be a prolific breeder, and under the sheltered conditions where it lives, it breeds throughout the year. Litters consist of five to ten young and a female may produce five or six litters in the space of a year. Females commence breeding at three months old and the gestation period is about four weeks.

ORDER RODENTIA

Family Gliridae

Dormice

Woodland dormouse

Graphiurus murinus

Boswaaierstertmuis

Distribution: Specimens of the woodland dormouse have been found in woodland areas throughout the Park, but it is apparently not a common species.
Habitat: In the Park they are found in savanna woodland, where they make

use of hollow trees and crevices under loose bark to lie up during the daylight hours.

Habits: These small nocturnal animals look rather like miniature squirrels but have a mouse-like anatomy. They are arboreal, living in woodland and dry forests, but they also frequent human habitation, where they invade the roofs of buildings or huts. On occasion, the dried leaves of tree aloes are utilised as day-time refuges. Hot veld fires take a heavy toll of these rodents when many of their hollow-tree refuges are destroyed. Their characteristic features are their bushy tails, soft fur and large eyes.

Diet: Dormice have a fairly omnivorous diet, consisting mainly of vegetable matter and seeds, but they also take insects and appear to be particularly fond of millipedes such as the large, black-and-yellow *Doratogonus flavifilis* which they kill in considerable numbers. The remnants of these millipedes in a pile near the entrance-hole of a hollow tree is a sure sign that a dormouse is about.

Breeding: A female with three small foetuses has been taken in February but not much else is known of their breeding habits.

Woodland dormouse

ORDER LAGOMORPHA

Family Leporidae

Hares and rabbits

Cape hare

Lepus capensis

Vlakhaas

Distribution: So far, the Cape hare is known in the Park from only two specimens which were collected near Shingomeni on the eastern boundary north of Shingwedzi Rest Camp and at Nwambiya Pan. More intensive surveys may prove that this species has a wider distribution in the eastern regions of the Park, although there are very few confirmed records of the Cape hare's occurrence in the savanna woodlands of southern Africa.

Habitat: It favours grassland, tending to utilise more open habitat than the scrub hare although occurring marginally on the same ground in some parts, for example, where scattered scrub bushes in grass favour both species.

Cape hare

Scrub hare

Habits: Like the scrub hare the Cape hare is nocturnal, lying low during the day, often in very scanty cover where it is nonetheless difficult to see. It relies mainly on its cryptic colouration to escape detection, but will dart away at high speed when flushed. It has been noted that the colour of the coat varies according to the habitat. In the Makgadikgadi area of Botswana, for instance, where the sand is white, Cape hares are much lighter in colour than elsewhere. Adult Cape hares usually have a mass of just over 1,5 kilograms. The life-span is about five years.
Diet: Cape hares subsist almost entirely on grass and prefer to feed in areas of short grass.
Breeding: They normally occur singly, although during mating one or more males may compete for a female. The gestation period is about 42 days. Two young are usually born, although triplets are occasionally recorded. They are born fully haired with their eyes open. Breeding takes place throughout the year, with a birth peak during the summer.

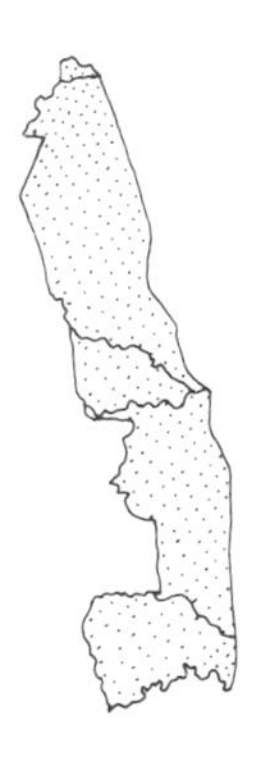

Scrub hare *Lepus saxatilis*

Kolhaas

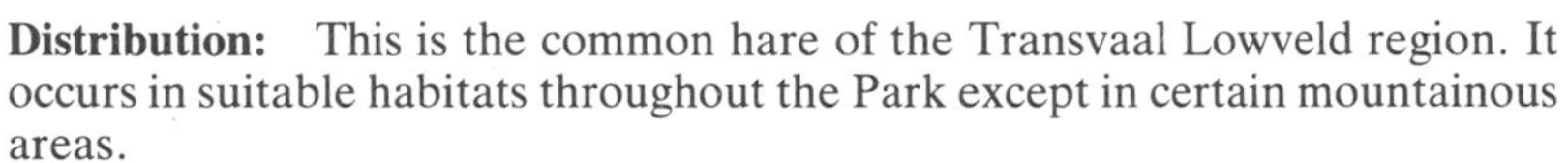

Distribution: This is the common hare of the Transvaal Lowveld region. It occurs in suitable habitats throughout the Park except in certain mountainous areas.
Habitat: In general it has a very wide habitat tolerance throughout its range but is absent from certain montane areas and forests. In the Park it is usually associated with savannas and grassland as long as there is some grass cover. It is also common in the mopane savannas.
Habits: The scrub hare is a nocturnal species like most other hares. It hides in suitable shelters under thick scrub or bushes by day and emerges at night to feed on surrounding grasslands or cultivated lands and gardens, where it can cause extensive damage. It is frequently attracted to the short green grass on the edges of roads and it is often seen during night-driving, caught in the beam of a car's headlights (particularly in the dry season). Like others of its kin it is not easily flushed by day from its form, and dashes off only at the last moment. It may be distinguished from other African hares by its large size and long ears. There is usually a patch of white fur on the forehead which gives it its Afrikaans name ("kol" = spot). It also lacks the yellowish line where the dorsal and ventral colours meet, a feature typical of the Cape hare. The scrub hare is a fast and elusive runner and runs in a jinking manner to

escape pursuers. On open roads it is blinded by the headlights of cars and considerable numbers are killed at night in this way. Adult specimens attain a mass of between 2,0 and 3,0 kilograms in the Transvaal, considerably more than the Cape hare.
Diet: The scrub hare's diet consists almost entirely of grass.
Breeding: The young are born in thick cover throughout the year but with a birth peak during summer. The gestation period is approximately one month. One to three young are produced to a litter and, like the leverets of the Cape hare, are born fully haired with their eyes open and capable of active movement.

Natal red hare *Pronolagus crassicaudatus*

Natalse rooihaas

Distribution: The Natal red hare is the largest of the three red hare species in southern Africa; in the Park it is strictly confined to the mountainous and broken sandstone hill country north of the Punda Maria/Pafuri road as well as to the sandstone outcrops between the Luvuvhu and Limpopo rivers. Although this species has been collected at Legogote, near White River, it has not yet been recorded in the mountainous areas between Pretoriuskop and Malelane.
Habitat: It is confined in the Park to areas of rocky koppies, hills and ravines in the sandstone belt of the far north. An additional habitat requirement is some grass or shrub cover.
Habits: These conspicuously coloured hares lie up during the day in characteristic shallow depressions under rocks, or in thick vegetation in rocky terrain. They are, in consequence, not often seen, being nocturnal and emerging only after dark to feed in open grassy patches adjoining their forms. Their presence in an area can be detected by their distinctive flattened, pellet-like droppings which are deposited in middens. Their major enemies are leopards and black eagles and when startled, they utter rather loud squeals as they dash away. They also scream pathetically when caught or wounded. Adult specimens may attain a mass of just over 2 kilograms.
Diet: Like other hare species the Natal red hare feeds mainly on grasses and appears to prefer young green shoots.
Breeding: Very little is known of the breeding biology of this species. Usually two young are born to a litter.

Natal red hare

Four-toed elephant-shrew

Short-snouted elephant-shrew

ORDER
MACROSCELIDEA

Family
Macroscelididae

Elephant-shrews

Four-toed elephant-shrew

Petrodromus tetradactylus

Bosklaasneus

Distribution: These large and strikingly coloured elephant-shrews are relatively common in suitable habitats. Their range is restricted to the Punda Maria and Pafuri sections of the northern district. The local records were the first for the species within the boundaries of the Transvaal although they also occur in north-eastern Natal.
Habitat: They appear to prefer dry as well as riparian forests with dense underbush and thickets.
Habits: Four-toed elephant-shrews are interesting insectivores with long, tapering snouts which wiggle and twitch as they sniff the air. They are very agile and, when disturbed or in a hurry, flee in hops and leaps by means of the elongated hindlegs, rather like miniature kangaroos. Normally they will walk on all fours when routing for food amongst organic debris, and they can also run on all four feet. They follow established routes, and their saltatorial (= jumping) mode of locomotion results in these routes consisting of a meandering series of bare patches (= landing-places) amongst the ground litter. Four-toed elephant-shrews are predominantly nocturnal and observations indicate that they are solitary when hunting for food. They are often observed to drum the ground with their hindfeet, but it is not certain whether this is a sign of agitation or an attempt to disturb subsurface insects. They rest up in shallow burrows under the exposed roots of trees, holes, rock crevices, under logs or in holes in termite-mounds.
Diet: The four-toed elephant-shrew is insectivorous and feeds largely on insects and their larvae, including termites and ants.
Breeding: A single nursling was found under a loose boulder in broken country during January. Scant observations from elsewhere in the Southern African Subregion indicate that their breeding season coincides with summer. One, and occasionally two young are born per litter. The young are precocial and are born fully haired and with their eyes open.

Short-snouted elephant-shrew

Elephantulus brachyrhynchus

Kortneusklaasneus

Distribution: The short-snouted elephant-shrew has been recorded from the northern, central and southern districts of the Park, and probably occurs in suitable habitat throughout the area.

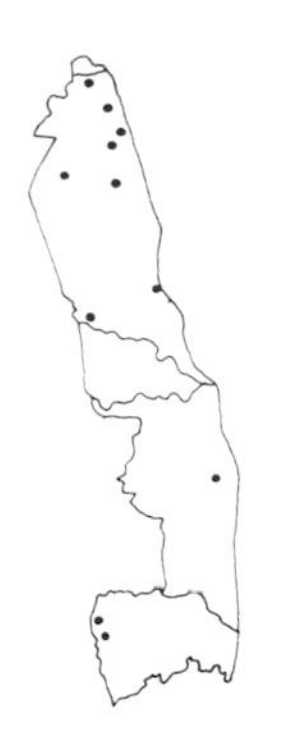

Habitat: They inhabit savanna woodland plains with dense substrate cover.
Habits: Short-snouted elephant-shrews live in shallow burrows and are almost entirely diurnal. They appear to be mainly solitary and may sometimes be seen in their well-used "runs" which meander through the grass and scattered bushes. When running they often make erratic jumps and, on stopping, drum their hindfeet.
Diet: Specimens have been trapped on bait consisting of peanut butter, mixed with fragments of meat. This attracts large numbers of ants and it is believed that the elephant-shrews are attracted more by the ants than by the peanut butter. They are known to feed on myrmecine ants such as *Pheidole megacephala* and termites such as *Hodotermes* spp. They have also been recorded to feed on vegetable matter and seeds in East Africa; in captivity they will accept a variety of insects.
Breeding: A female recovered from the stomach of an African wild cat in February carried two full-term foetuses. Four out of five pregnant females collected during summer carried twins. The fifth had only one foetus.

Rock elephant-shrew

Rock elephant-shrew

Elephantulus myurus

Klipklaasneus

Distribution: The rock elephant-shrew is a montane form confined to the Lebombo mountain range north of Olifantspoort and the broken hill country north of the Punda Maria/Pafuri road.
Habitat: The rock elephant-shrew is fairly common in rocky surroundings offering suitable crevices and crannies which are utilised for safe shelter. It is found particularly around the edges of Lebombo-ironwood communities.
Habits: The species is predominantly crepuscular (that is, it is active during the twilight hours), although trapping results indicate that there is some degree of both diurnal and nocturnal activity. It tends to keep to the shady cover of overhanging rocks or bushes but ventures into bright sunlit areas with quick, darting movements. Individuals have been observed sunning themselves during late afternoons on the edges of rocks, rather like dassies.
Diet: They feed on small insects, especially ants and termites, and often forage for such food items in dassie middens.
Breeding: Gravid females (occasionally with only one foetus, mostly with two but never with more) have been recorded from September to April.

SELECTED SOURCES OF REFERENCES

ANSELL, W.F.H. 1978. *The mammals of Zambia*. National Parks and Wildlife Service, Chilanga, Zambia.

BOSMAN, P. & HALL-MARTIN, A. 1986. *Elephants of Africa*. C. Struik, Cape Town.

BOTHMA, J. DU P. 1971. Part 12: Order Hyracoidea. In: *The mammals of Africa: an identification manual*. (Eds.) Meester, J. & Setzer, H.W. Smithsonian Institution Press, Washington D.C.

BRYNARD, A.M. & PIENAAR, U. de V. 1960. Annual report of the Biologist, 1958/1959. *Koedoe* 3:1-205.

COETZEE, C.G. 1963. The prey of owls in the Kruger National Park as indicated by owl pellets collected during 1960-61. *Koedoe* 6:115-125.

COETZEE, C.G. 1977. Part 8: Order Carnivora, main text. In: *The mammals of Africa: an identification manual*. (Eds.) Meester, J. & Setzer, H.W. Smithsonian Institution Press, Washington D.C.

DAVIS, D.H.S. 1959. The barn owl's contribution to ecology and palaeoecology. *The Ostrich Supplement* 3:144-153.

DAVIS, D.H.S. 1962. Distribution patterns of southern African Muridae, with notes on some of their fossil antecedents. *Ann. Cape Prov. Mus*. 2:56-76.

DE GRAAFF, G. 1962. On the nest of *Cryptomys hottentotus* in the Kruger National Park. *Koedoe* 5:157-161.

DE GRAAFF, G. 1975. Part 6.9: Family Bathyergidae. In: *The mammals of Africa: an identification manual*. (Eds.) Meester, J. & Setzer, H.W. Smithsonian Institution Press, Washington D.C.

DE GRAAFF, G. 1981. *The rodents of southern Africa*. Butterworths, Durban.

DIXON, J.E.W. 1966. Notes on the mammals of the Ndumu Game Reserve. *The Lammergeyer* 6:24-40.

DORST, J. & DANDELOT, P. 1983. *A field guide to the larger mammals of Africa*. Collins, London.

ELLERMAN, J.R., MORRISON-SCOTT, T.C.S. & HAYMAN, R.W. 1953. *Southern African mammals 1758 to 1951: a reclassification*. Trustees of the British Museum (Nat. Hist.), London.

FENTON, M.B. 1983. *Just bats*. University of Toronto Press, Toronto.

FENTON, M.B. 1985. *Communication in the Chiroptera*. Indiana University Press, Bloomington.

GERTENBACH, W.P.D. 1983. Landscapes of the Kruger National Park. *Koedoe* 26:9-121.

HALTENORTH, T. & DILLER, H. 1984. *A field guide to the mammals of Africa including Madagascar*. Collins, London.

HAYMAN, R.W. & HILL, J.E. 1971. Part 2: Order Chiroptera. In: *The mammals of Africa: an identification manual*. (Eds.) Meester, J. & Setzer, H.W. Smithsonian Institution Press, Washington D.C.

HILL, J.E. & SMITH, J.D. 1984. *Bats, a natural history*. University of Texas Press, Austin.

HONACKI, J.H., KINMAN, K.E. & KOEPPL, J.W. (eds.).1982. *Mammal species of the world: a taxonomic and geographic reference*. Allen Press and the Association of Systematics Collections, Lawrence, Kansas.

KERN, N.G. 1977. *The influence of fire on populations of small mammals of the Kruger National Park*. Unpublished M.Sc. thesis, Pretoria University, Pretoria.

MABERLY, C.T. ASTLEY. 1963. *The game animals of southern Africa*. Thomas Nelson & Sons, Johannesburg.

MEESTER, J.A.J. 1963. A systematic revision of the shrew genus *Crocidura* in southern Africa. *Transvaal Museum Memoir* 13:1-127.

MEESTER, J.A.J. 1972. A new golden mole from the Transvaal (Mammalia: Chrysochloridae). *Annals of the Transvaal Museum* 28(4):35-46.

MEESTER, J. & SETZER, H.W. (eds.) 1971. *The mammals of Africa: an identification manual*. Smithsonian Institution Press, Washington D.C.

MEESTER, J.A.J., RAUTENBACH, I.L., DIPPENAAR, N.J. & BAKER, C. 1986. Classification of Southern African Mammals. *Transvaal Museum Monograph* 5:1-359.

MISONNE, X. 1974. Part 6: Order Rodentia, main text. In: *The mammals of Africa: an identification manual*. (Eds.) Meester, J. & Setzer, H.W. Smithsonian Institution Press, Washington D.C.

PETTER, F. 1971. Part 5: Order Lagomorpha. In: *The mammals of Africa: an identification manual*. (Eds.) Meester, J. & Setzer, H.W. Smithsonian Institution Press, Washington D.C.

PIENAAR, U. de V. 1963. The large mammals of the Kruger National Park – their distribution and present-day status. *Koedoe* 6:1-37.

PIENAAR, U. de V. 1964. The small mammals of the Kruger National Park – a systematic list and zoogeography. *Koedoe* 7:1-25.

PIENAAR, U. de V. 1970. A note on the occurrence of bat-eared fox *Otocyon megalotis megalotis* (Desmarest) in the Kruger National Park. *Koedoe* 13:23-27.

PIENAAR, U. de V. 1972. A new bat record for the Kruger National Park. *Koedoe* 15:91-93.

PIENAAR, U. de V. 1978. *The reptile fauna of the Kruger National Park*. National Parks Board of Trustees, Pretoria.

PIENAAR, U. de V. 1978. *The freshwater fishes of the Kruger National Park*. National Parks Board of Trustees, Pretoria.

PIENAAR, U. de V., PASSMORE, N.I. & CARRUTHERS, V.C. 1976. *The frogs of the Kruger National Park*. National Parks Board of Trustees, Pretoria.

PIENAAR, U. de V., RAUTENBACH, I.L. & DE GRAAFF, G. 1980. *The small mammals of the Kruger National Park*. National Parks Board of Trustees, Pretoria.

RASA, A. 1985. *Mongoose watch: a family observed*. John Murray, London.

RAUTENBACH, I.L. 1975. Another new bat record for the Kruger National Park. *Koedoe* 18:203-204.

RAUTENBACH, I.L. 1978. Ecological distribution of the mammals of the Transvaal (Vertebrata: Mammalia). *Annals of the Transvaal Museum* 31(10):131-156.

RAUTENBACH, I.L., DE GRAAFF, G. & PIENAAR, U. de V. 1979. Records of seven small mammal species (Insectivora, Chiroptera) new to the Kruger National Park. *Koedoe* 22:81-87.

RAUTENBACH, I.L. 1982. Mammals of the Transvaal. *Ecoplan Monograph* 1:1-211. (Ecoplan, Pretoria).

RAUTENBACH, I.L. & ESPIE, I.W. 1982. First records of occurrence for two species of bats in the Kruger National Park. *Koedoe* 25:111-112.

RAUTENBACH, I.L., SCHLITTER, D.A. & BRAACK, L.E.O. 1984. New distributional records of bats for the Republic of South Africa, with special reference to the Kruger National Park. *Koedoe* 27:131-135.

RAUTENBACH, I.L., FENTON, M.B. & BRAACK, L.E.O. 1985. First records of five species of insectivorous bats from the Kruger National Park. *Koedoe* 28:73-80.

ROBERTS, A. 1951. *The mammals of South Africa*. Trustees of "The Mammals of South Africa" Book Fund, Johannesburg.

ROWE-ROWE, D.T. 1978. The small carnivores of Natal. *The Lammergeyer* 25:1-48.

SANDENBERGH, J.A.B. 1946-1952. Annual reports of the warden of the Kruger National Park. Unpublished reports, National Parks Board, Pretoria.

SCHLITTER, D.A. & RAUTENBACH, I.L. 1977. The occurrence of the aloe bat *Eptesicus zuluensis* in the Kruger National Park. *Koedoe* 20:187-188.

SHORTRIDGE, G.C. 1934, *The mammals of South West Africa*. Vols. 1 & 2. William Heinemann, London.

SMITHERS, R.H.N. 1966. *The mammals of Rhodesia, Zambia and Malawi*. Collins, London.

SMITHERS, R.H.N. 1968. *A check list and atlas of the mammals of Botswana (Africa)*. Trustees of the National Museums of Rhodesia, Salisbury.

SMITHERS, R.H.N. 1975. *Guide to the rats and mice of Rhodesia*. Trustees of the National Museums and Monuments of Rhodesia, Salisbury.

SMITHERS, R.H.N. 1983. *The mammals of the Southern African Subregion*. University of Pretoria, Pretoria.

SMITHERS, R.H.N. 1986, South African Red Data Book – terrestrial mammals. *South African National Scientific Programmes Report* 125:1-214.

SMITHERS, R.H.N. 1986. *Land mammals of southern Africa: a field guide*. Macmillan South Africa, Johannesburg.

SMITHERS, R.H.N. & LOBÂO TELLO, J.L.P. 1976. Check list and atlas of the mammals of Moçambique. *Museum Memoir* 8:1-184. (Trustees of the National Museums and Monuments of Rhodesia, Salisbury).

SMITHERS, R.H.N. & WILSON, V.J. 1979. Check list and atlas of the mammals of Zimbabwe Rhodesia. *Museum Memoir* 9:1-193. (Trustees of the National Museums and Monuments of Zimbabwe Rhodesia, Salisbury).

SMUTS, G.L. 1982. *Lion*. Macmillan South Africa, Johannesburg.

STEVENSON-HAMILTON, J. 1947 *Wildlife in South Africa*. Cassel & Co. Ltd., London.

STEVENSON-HAMILTON, J. 1902-1945. Annual reports of the warden of the Kruger National Park. Unpublished reports, National Parks Board, Pretoria.

WALKER, C. 1986. *Signs of the wild*. C. Struik, Cape Town.

WILSON, V.J. 1975. Mammals of the Wankie National Park, Rhodesia. *Museum Memoir* 5:1-147. (Trustees of the National Museums and Monuments of Rhodesia, Salisbury).

Albinism. A condition characterized by a congenital absence or deficiency of colouring pigment in the skin, hair and eyes.

Arboreal. Adapted for life in trees.

Brisket. Breast of a mammal.

Browser (see also 'grazer'). An animal that feeds predominantly on the leaves, twigs or shoots of shrubs and trees.

Catholic (diet). Universal; all-embracing; wide.

Commensalism. A situation in which members of different species live in close association without much mutual influence and share the same food resource.

Crepuscular. Active during the twilight hours of dusk and dawn.

Cryptic (of colouration or behaviour of animals). Tending to conceal by disguising or camouflaging the shape.

Diurnal. Active during daylight hours.

Endemic. Native to, and restricted to, a particular geographic region.

Enzootic. A disease occurring in a given animal species within a limited geographical area.

Forb. A broad-leaved herbaceous plant (not a grass).

Fossorial. Adapted for burrowing into the soil and for life in such burrows.

Gallery forest. A narrow strip of forest along the banks of a river in an otherwise sparsely wooded landscape.

Gravid. Pregnant.

Grazer (see also 'browser'). An animal cropping the surface growth of herbs and particularly grasses.

Hermaphrodite. Bisexual; having both male and female reproductive organs in the same animal.

Holt. Animal's (especially otter's) lair or den.

Indigenous. Native to a particular area.

Lactating. Secreting milk from the mammary glands.

Leveret. Young hare up to one year old.

Melanistic. An increase over normal in the amount of black or dark pigment in the skin of an animal, population or group.

Oestrus (adj. 'oestrous'). The period of maximum sexual receptivity, or heat, in female mammals, usually coinciding with the release of eggs from the ovaries.

Omnivorous. Feeding on a mixed diet of plant and animal material.

Perennial (of a river). Flowing through all seasons of the year.

Polygamous. Pertaining to the condition in which a single male has several female mates at any one time.

Polyoestrous (of female mammals). Coming into oestrus or heat more than once in a season.

Saltatorial. Pertaining to, or adapted for, leaping or bounding locomotion.

Scat. An animal faecal dropping.

Sedentary. Inactive or non-migrating life-style.

Serotine. Late. Originally applied as a common name to a European bat species which flies late in the evening; now used as a common name for related species in the genus *Eptesicus* elsewhere in the world.

Sounder. Herd of wild pigs.

Sympatric. Populations or species occurring together in the same geographical area.

Terrestrial. Pertaining to, or living habitually on, the land or ground surface.

Vivarium. Enclosure artificially prepared for keeping animals in conditions approximating their natural state.

W.N.L.A. Witwatersrand Native Labour Association.

INDEX TO SCIENTIFIC NAMES

INDEX TO AFRIKAANS NAMES